50 YEARS

SAGE was founded in 1965 by Sara Miller McCune to support the dissemination of usable knowledge by publishing innovative and high-quality research and teaching content. Today, we publish more than 850 journals, including those of more than 300 learned societies, more than 800 new books per year, and a growing range of library products including archives, data, case studies, reports, conference highlights, and video. SAGE remains majority-owned by our founder, and after Sara's lifetime will become owned by a charitable trust that secures our continued independence.

Los Angeles | London | New Delhi | Singapore | Washington DC

Advance Praise

The Magnetic Organization: Attracting and Retaining the Best Talent written by Professor Dipak Kumar Bhattacharyya, a well-acclaimed name in the field of human resource management, is for the HR practitioner who is seeking a "go-to," "how-to" book on attracting and retaining winners. Based on sound theoretical principles, with industry examples and step-by-step action plans, it will be an invaluable aid to any manager who wants to emerge as a winner in today's "war for talent."

Snigdha Pattnaik, Dean, Xavier School of HRM,
Xavier University, Bhubaneswar

Professor Dipak Kumar Bhattacharyya is a well-known scholar in talent management practices in organizations and a gifted writer whose enormous experience in both the academic and corporate world blends together both theory and practice in distilling the core essence of TM's value proposition and suggesting the tools and techniques for acquiring and retaining talent. One of the book's key strengths lies in its comprehensiveness in terms of its orientation, style, coherence, coverage, and depth, replete with tips, illustrative examples, and cases—one that makes effortless and stimulating reading. I am sure this book will help both HR practitioners and students with a compelling value proposition to wide readership both in India and abroad in winning the "war for talent."

Professor K. Trivikram,
Institute of Public Enterprise, Hyderabad

The title of the book *The Magnetic Organization: Attracting and Retaining the Best Talent* obviously grabbed my attention, as its theme is of contemporary relevance. Dr Bhattacharyya, a professor in Xavier University, Bhubaneswar, is a renowned scholar and a passionate teacher. This book encompasses a unique blend of theory and virtual applications to study organizational dynamics, embedded with strategic plans to accomplish talent management for effective acquisition and retention of talent in organizations. I strongly believe this book will serve as a guide to the manifold challenges of an organization toward achieving the status of "The Magnetic Employer." I wish the book all success.

Fr. Antony Uvari, S.J., Registrar,
Xavier University, Bhubaneswar

The most successful companies now practice talent management to maintain their competitive advantage. Professor Dipak Kumar Bhattacharyya's new book has captured strategies and proven practices to build a world class workforce.

Howard Risher, Pay and Performance Consultant and
Editor, *Compensation & Benefits Review*

I greatly value this book from two standpoints: First attracting and retaining the best talent is one of the biggest challenges for organizations. Professor Bhattacharyya has vividly emphasized the value of talent, developing talent and retaining the talent. He has also gone into many well-known theories and concepts related to talent development. In the process, he also suggested various strategies to develop and retain talent. Second, the book will be very useful to Human Resource professionals, researchers, and organizations in their recruitment and further in developing and retaining talent.

Dr Raj Agrawal, Director, Centre for Management
Education, All India Management Association

With the fierce competitions and economics difficulties, it becomes more and more important for organizations to build knowledge assets as quickly and flexibly as possible. One solution before organizations is becoming "talent magnets." This book tackles the gap between established theories and practices on talent management and provides step-by-step action plans to talent acquisition and retaining through in-house capabilities. The author in his book *The Magnetic Organization: Attracting and Retaining the Best Talent* simplifies and synthesizes issues, including controversial ones and provides new insights on talent management. The author's approach makes the book suitable for talent management courses as well as a self-guide for organization's managers.

Latif Al-Hakim, Associate Professor,
University of Southern Queensland, Australia

Ever since the phrase "War for Talent" became a part of the HR manager's dictionary, there have been numerous seminars and discussions on the topic. However, I think for the first time Professor Dipak Bhattacharyya has succeeded in providing a comprehensive road map to win the war! His concept of an employer as a talent magnet captures very succinctly today's needs of organizations vis-à-vis talent management. This book will be helpful to all those with a serious interest in talent management

Arunav Banerjee, Program Chair and Professor,
Human Resources Leadership Program,
School of Inspired Leadership, Gurgaon

The
Magnetic
Organization

The Magnetic Organization

Attracting and Retaining the Best Talent

Dipak Kumar Bhattacharyya

www.sagepublications.com

Los Angeles • London • New Delhi • Singapore • Washington DC

First published in 2015 by

SAGE Response
B1/I-1 Mohan Cooperative Industrial Area
Mathura Road, New Delhi 110 044, India

SAGE Publications Inc
2455 Teller Road
Thousand Oaks, California 91320, USA

SAGE Publications Ltd
1 Oliver's Yard, 55 City Road
London EC1Y 1SP, United Kingdom

SAGE Publications Asia-Pacific Pte Ltd
3 Church Street
#10-04 Samsung Hub
Singapore 049483

Published by Vivek Mehra for SAGE Publications India Pvt Ltd, typeset in 11/13 Bembo by RECTO Graphics, Delhi and printed at Chaman Enterprises, New Delhi.

Library of Congress Cataloging-in-Publication Data Available

ISBN: 978-93-515-0387-3 (PB)

The SAGE Team: Sachin Sharma, Vandana Gupta, Rajib Chatterjee, and Rajinder Kaur

To my wife and children

Thank you for choosing a SAGE product!
If you have any comment, observation or feedback,
I would like to personally hear from you.
Please write to me at **contactceo@sagepub.in**

Vivek Mehra, Managing Director and CEO, SAGE India.

Bulk Sales

SAGE India offers special discounts
for purchase of books in bulk.
We also make available special imprints
and excerpts from our books on demand.

For orders and enquiries, write to us at

Marketing Department
SAGE Publications India Pvt Ltd
B1/I-1, Mohan Cooperative Industrial Area
Mathura Road, Post Bag 7
New Delhi 110044, India

E-mail us at **marketing@sagepub.in**

Get to know more about SAGE

Be invited to SAGE events, get on our mailing list.
Write today to **marketing@sagepub.in**

This book is also available as an e-book.

Contents

Preface

The biggest challenge enterprises face today is attracting and retaining talent. A company becomes a magnetic organization when:

- it attracts the best of talent;
- applicants are eager to work for the company;
- people envy its employees;
- it receives unsolicited resumes; and
- talented workers stay with the company throughout their careers.

Even if most companies succeed in attracting the best talent, most of them falter on the critical part which is retention. When a talented employee leaves the organization, the entire cycle of recruitment, training, and development is repeated. Not only this, but also when an individual resigns from his present organization, it is more likely that he would join the competitors. In such cases, employees tend to take all the strategies and policies from the current organization to the new one.

Attracting and retaining the best talent by becoming a magnetic employer requires us to believe that with a talent-driven approach we can sustain and grow. Then, of course, we need to redefine and redesign our people management practices with a changed perspective. Certain terms need to be replaced and certain need to be added, to reflect that we believe in talent, we value talent, we develop talent, we retain talent, and finally we attract talent. We are a magnetic employer.

A magnetic organization is a talent magnet. Such an employer can attract and retain talent. Employers who are not magnetic become talent repulsive. With magnetic power, organizations gain strength and see the beeline of talent—be it in the campuses or job fairs. With the exponential power of recruiting, organizations get the best available talent from the market, and can also retain them, as employees feel more and more engaged and committed to the organizations. They gradually relate themselves with the organizations, establish their identity, and enjoy their sense of pride, as they are working for the best organizations. Such employees also become talent attractors, as prospects emulate their steps in joining the organizations. Hence, the power of magnetic employer multiplies, with more and more talents making a beeline to increase the talent pool. An employer, therefore, becomes a talent magnet: first for its organizational branding and second for its employees who create a pull effect with a compelling message that they are working with the best-fit organizations that not only attract talents, but also nurture them, develop them, and make all-out efforts to retain them.

Could we make use of storytelling? Our stories can help in building our brand identity. Similarly, put our all-out endeavors to transform our employees as talent magnets. This will make our organizations more and more magnetic to pull the talent. This will make our organizational talent management (TM) cycle self-reinforcing, and drive our organization to achieve long-term sustainability and growth. What strategies are required for these? The chief executive officers (CEOs) may have their individual preferences. We may not get any commonality or even any universality in their approaches. Many, however, contended with a mindset to question our strategies and actions; it is possible to take incremental and corrective steps, which can gradually transform our organizations into a magnetic employer.

Social media today often goes against our hard-earned magnetic power. For years, Siemens had to struggle to recuperate from the bribery slur of marketing people to get orders from their customers and prove that they are a good organization. Make your presence felt in the social media, contradict negative publicity, develop your own stories, and tell those regularly. Make your followers believe that you are the best.

We do not have any quick-fix solution to develop organization as a magnetic employer, but by answering the following questions, perhaps we can get a direction:

- How attractive is your workplace?
- What can pull talents to your organization?
- Could you make your workplace a compelling place to work?
- What benefits do we provide to our employees?
- What can make our employees work and stay with us?
- What can transform your workplace to be more challenging?
- Could you showcase your employees' value proposition (EVP)?
- Are you diversity neutral?
- Do you have great stories to tell?
- Are you active on social media?
- Could you make your employees talent magnets?
- Could you feel that you are the talk of the market?
- Could you feel the cascading effect on the mindset of the customers, who started believing that your products and services are the best?

With answers to the above questions, we can deduce our magnetism and go on attracting and retaining talent. We can understand the power of magnetism when we are able to attract the best talent, people take interest in our company, people envy our employees, our employees choose to stay with our organization, and we start getting more and more unsolicited resumes.

Also, organizations can assess their magnetic power to attract and retain talent, when they become talk of the market not only for the people with talent to choose them as potential employers, but also for the consumers who might start feeling that the products and services of the companies are better than others. Similarly, such organizations can also retain, nurture, and develop talent, and can become more productive, and optimize the human resource costs. A high rate of talent retention obviously reduces the cost of manpower replacement (for re-recruitment) and also the cost of training (re-training of the replaced manpower).

Organizations can become magnetic employers by understanding the needs of the potential talent, and bringing similar culture in their work environment accordingly. It requires creating an EVP powered by the organizational values. EVP attracts the talent pool when the potential employees feel that the organization is special over others. Through social media, organizations try to engage with the talent pool, carrying the message that they are the best. While talent attraction is possible with such magnetic power, talent retention requires certain organizational practices. Such practices will make employees feel that they are with an organization that values talent with more inclusive approach, acknowledges their contribution to organizational growth, and makes available enough space for their growth and development. With such feelings, employees get more and more engaged and remain with the organization, even for the entire period of their work-life cycle.

This book unravels the process of making an organization "The Magnetic Employer" through efficient TM practices, encompassing the whole gamut of talent attraction, development, and retention. With a blended approach, the book combines the theories and practices, drawing lessons from the corporate world. With lessons on practices, step-by-step action plans, unlike other professional books, this book would be the best self-help guide for acquisition, development, and retention of talent, encompassing the entire cycle of TM.

Why This Book?

TM in organizations today faces new challenges. This is primarily for a paradigm shift in global business landscape. Business globalization, intense pressure of competition, economic turbulence, and changing percepts of human resources not only call for renewed attention to career management issues, but also emphasize on talent acquisition and retention. Talented people always look for new and emerging career opportunities, both within and outside their organizations. Professionally managed organizations, even though craft their career plans for employees effectively, fail to create career development opportunities, often due to business uncertainty. Even now very few organizations commit their investment for human capital development. In many cases, organizations operating globally, managing global careers, become another new challenge.

Solvay, the 150-year-old Belgium-based global chemical major, after acquisition of Rhodia of France, is now facing the real challenge of global career management. Acquisition of Rhodia has now substantially expanded businesses reach of Solvay to China and Southeast Asia, which earlier had minimum business share. Solvay manages its business through global business units (GBUs). To successfully leverage the advantage of high market growth opportunities, like Asia and Latin America, Solvay emphasizes on developing local talents for their GBUs. Solvay's corporate level manpower extends support to these local talents only for a short duration. Local talents then develop within the GBUs, facing the business realities of their own market environment. Unlike other multinationals, Solvay recognizes local talents not only with competitive rewards, but also by providing excellent career development opportunities. Such an approach to global talent management is even not observed in many Japanese organizations operating in India.

Talent is an inherent potentiality of all of us. It is for the organization to recognize, nurture, develop, motivate, and retain talent. I keep track on B-school graduates selected through campus for my client organizations. The idea behind this is to validate our recruitment decisions in terms of their performance, development, and potentiality for future leadership roles. Our recruitment decisions are not always right; often we find that we ultimately end up with clever-fools. Clever-fools are apparently clever; hence, you cannot assess them, and you can only understand them in action. We experimented with all TM advices, tips on attraction and retention, but nothing yielded any lasting results. One of my client organizations lamented that all their investment in grooming in-house talent became futile, as a couple of them had joined the rival organizations. They now lay their golden eggs with them. "We decided to scrap our succession plans. Rather saving on this, we can source talent directly from competing organizations with premium compensation and rewards." "Never do that" was my advice. "Rather investigate, why people are leaving."

In a reverse tracking of B-school graduates, whom my clients rejected for their poor interview performance or failure in one or more interview components, to my surprise, I find that today, a couple of them carry a high price tag for their talents. My clients even laterally recruited them at a premium price. What was wrong in tracking them early? This is why this book is so worthy. The instant case is funny. Some of the B-school graduates were not selected in campus interview because they miserably transpired to be individualistic in companies' mandated psychometric tests. "We value team work; hence we cannot make entry for individualistic people." Fine, but who designed these psychometric tests? Are they reliable and validated? With all answers also, somehow, I was not convinced. Are we wrong anywhere? Perhaps the answer is not one, but multiple, as we take a journey through this book.

This book is not intended to debate on TM literatures, rather more focused on TM's value proposition and suggesting the tools and techniques for acquiring and retaining talent. Acquiring and retaining talent is a strategic imperative for every organization to sustain in competition. Ed Michaels, Helen Handfield-Jones, and Beth Axelrod, the trio of McKinsey in their "War for Talent" had argued that talent acquisition and retention is not just limited to recruitment and motivation. It goes beyond, as organizations have to work out robust strategies for attraction, development, and retention of talented people, even if it requires changes in policies, systems, and structures. It is literal change in perspectives of organizations from human resource to human capital.

Human capital concept per se is a transition from control to commitment approach. Organizations invest in human capital to get incremental change in their business results. Often organizations use the term human capital management interchangeably with TM. Viewing people as a resource for the organization embeds our mindset of exploitation. Contrarily viewing people as capital legitimizes our investment on people. We exploit resources including human resources to maximize our gains, while we invest on people to build their capabilities to perpetuate our sustenance. However, we have criticism on human capital approach too. People being considered non-expandable asset for the organization, like any other asset, can be owned, bought, sold, or traded. From organizational perspective, when human capital approach is followed, people can be reduced to inert disposable asset, when they fail to deliver expected level of performance. Like any other asset human capital value in an organization can also appreciate or depreciate. Hence, today our people may add value to our business for the talent they posses, but tomorrow they may not, unless we focus on nurturing and developing their talent, investing in human capital.

Organizations today realize that traditional human resource management practices, restricting investment on people, and managing them more as a cost to the organization, can no longer help them to sustain in competition. While human resource cost optimization is important, it cannot be the sole objective of HR professionals for incremental business gains. Thinking for long term requires our investment in attracting, developing, and retaining talent. And this can only ensure our sustainability, prevent our organization from becoming a corporate dinosaur.

Creation of EVP, long-term recruitment strategy, factoring coaching, mentoring, and experiences to develop in-house talent, and strengthening of talent through investment are recommended TM practices for organizations. However, its implementation requires adherence to rigorous stepped processes for acquisition and retention of talent in organizations. Anchoring the talent pool of our organizations first requires us to develop a shared conviction that talent can only ensure our sustainability, strengthening our competitive advantages. Talent is the critical driver of our business. It can propel our journey through uncertainty. Hence, investment in talent (both for acquisition and retention) is legitimate.

Deloitte's recent studies on Global Human Capital Trends (2014) put talent acquisition, retention, and management issues as one of the top four issues across the globe. The other three important issues, like leadership, retention and engagement, re-skilling the HR function, etc., when we examine carefully, are also attributable to TM issues. Similar studies by many other global consulting organizations, professional bodies, and institutions put talent on their topmost agenda for their sustenance and growth.

Indian organizations, managers, and HR professionals require more cost-effective solutions to TM. Hiring a consultant is cost prohibitive. Moreover, Indian business dynamics are different.

With maximum population in young age-group, challenge for TM is characteristically different from many industrially advanced countries.

The Book Design

This book is crafted based on author's long experience as an HR professional, teaching, and research, offering solutions to talent acquisition and retention through in-house capabilities. While the book owes heavily to the theoretical literatures across the globe, its conceptualization is leaned toward developing economies, like India and others. Unlike other professional books, this book espouses more applications than theories, and suggests step-by-step action plans for TM for effective acquisition and retention of talent through following chapters.

Chapter 1 discusses the definitions and concepts of talent, and also introduces various terms related to talent, talent attraction, talents acquisition, talent retention, talent development, talent management, talent pipeline, etc. This introductory chapter sets the premise for subsequent four chapters of the book. The chapter acknowledged the wide gap that exists between theories and practices on TM. Even on terminological issues, we have major differences among scholars. Although organizational practices differ in terms of individual business focus and strategies, we also observe cross-country differences in TM issues. The introductory chapter is expected to provide clarity on the definitions, concepts, and practices of talent and TM.

Chapter 2 of the book details talent acquisition. Talent acquisition is an ongoing process that aims to attract, find, and select highly talented individuals. It is strategically integrating learning and development and workforce planning functions of the organizations. Globally, organizations are innovative in their talent acquisition practices. Apart from acquiring talents through new recruitment, many organizations also focus on developing in-house talent pipeline, grooming people, after identifying their potentialities. Some companies are also acquiring talents through acquisition of companies. Talent analytics, dashboard, social networking sites, headhunting, brand building, organization-fit, job-fit analysis, etc., are some of the effective talent acquisition tools used by the organizations. Many organizations also use competency-based approach in acquiring talent.

Chapter 3 details talent development process, drawing inputs from theories and organizational practices, including the experiences of the author. Talent is scarce, and organizations across the world have to compete for talent. Hence, organizations have to continuously develop talent pacing with the changing business needs and strategies. The scope of talent development now extends to incubation of in-house talents. Holistic talent development requires developing a talent-driven organization culture. Talent pipeline in organizations has to meet both the present and future talent requirements of the organization. The chapter also focuses on the need for time-to-time calibration of talent development plans of the organizations, pacing with changing business plans and strategies.

Chapter 4 of the book deliberates on talent retention. The chapter starts with the discussion on the definitional debates on talent retention, and then investigates on possible TM practices, which can enhance talent retention for the organizations. Good organizations develop their specific talent retention strategies, and implement that right from day one of talent acquisition. Elaborate discussions on various talent retention tools and techniques, like employee engagement, career planning, and development, succession planning programs, workforce diversity, performance management systems, compensation and rewards programs, ambidextrous human resource management practices, etc., have been made theoretically, as well as drawing lessons from organizational practices.

Chapter 5 wraps up with elaborate discussions on TM issues, referring to talent management practices. All the preceding chapters discuss specific TM areas, like acquisition, retention, and development. As an integrated human resource management function, primary activities of TM are attracting, acquiring, developing, and retaining right people for the right job at the right time.

The chapter highlights the need for alignment of TM programs of the organizations with their business and strategies, for gaining the competitive advantages. For organizations that have presence across the globe, the chapter recommends the need for a global approach to TM. In cross-border mergers organizations are particularly facing the challenge of global talent management. The chapter also acknowledges the usefulness of talent analytics in managing talent, but warns it cannot altogether replace the subjective analysis.

Expectantly, the book will be a self-help guide to professionals for TM practices, which can help organizations to become "The Magnetic Employer." By becoming a magnetic employer, organizations can attract, acquire, and retain talent, which in the process, help in long-term growth and sustenance. For students, it would serve the purpose of a reference text. In many B-schools, TM is taught as a full credit course. We do not have any structured text on TM. This book can meet the requirement. For general readers, it would be a professional book to enrich their knowledge.

Acknowledgments

The author gratefully acknowledges time-to-time help and support from family members, friends, and professional colleagues. Also, the author is grateful to reviewers and editors of SAGE for timely help and support to bring out this book in the shortest possible time.

Bibliography

Global Human Capital Trends. (2014). *Engaging the 21st-Cetury workforce*. Deloitte University Press. Retrieved from http://d2mtr37y39tpbu.cloudfront.net/wp-content/uploads/2014/03/GlobalHumanCapitalTrends_2014.pdf (accessed on April 10, 2015).

Michaels, H. H.-J., & Axelrod, B. (2001). *The war for talent*. Boston, MA: Harvard Business School Press.

1

Introduction

Acquire the talent and nurture them to sustain in competition

With headcounts of 270,000 across 79 countries of the world and sales revenue of US$187.9 billion, Samsung is no doubt the global technology leader. Obviously such a company requires extraordinary talent to partner with their growth strategy. Attracting talent globally is always a major challenge for Samsung. Every time the company comes out with some innovative strategy. This time it is their "Launching People" program with world-class mentors from different walks of life. The idea is to find people with extraordinary ideas. Once such people are chosen, they are put under the mentors to collaborate on some unique project. Selection is done based on the screening of ideas received by these mentors.

But why is Samsung following this line of approach for talent acquisition? Reason is simple, Samsung wants to launch new products almost every day, which requires extraordinary talent. The company supports the passion and ambition of such people, and provides all technological support and infrastructure so that their ideas get shaped and bring out something new.

During talent acquisition the company also adopts a structured behavioral and skills-based interview process to ensure that the new hires are culture fit. The company does this to ensure job satisfaction and low employee turnover.

Samsung realizes that acquiring talent and then forgetting the need for nurturing cannot help them to sustain in competition. The company has extended the scope of talent development to all cross-sections of their employees, building their in-house capabilities. More than 50 percent of Samsung employees are in their 20s, hence without talent development support, the company is more

(Box continued)

1

(Box continued)

prone to manpower obsolescence. With educational planning and leadership training, the company could ensure holistic talent development for all cross-sections of employees. Such holistic approach to talent development even encompasses education and training on R&D, production technology, innovation, design, etc. In addition to the corporate level training and education support, the company has also created divisional and functional education units, so that all employees can be brought under their holistic talent development program.

Thus, with celebrities as mentor to new recruits, Samsung attracts the talent, and with in-house talent development support, the company nurtures them to remain best in the globally competitive market.

Talent is an inherent potentiality of all of us. It is for the organization to recognize, nurture, develop, motivate, and retain talent. We have many scholars who still believe talent is not our learned knowledge and skills; we possess it and sustain with it. Something that exists with us perennially, but can only be felt and understood by others, when we put people in action. Talent is hardware and software of our mind. While hardware is our acquired knowledge and skills; software is our cognition, which transforms to talent. Knowledge and skills provide us the strength, and cognition reflects our talent in the form of productive thoughts, feelings, and behavior. These are not mutually exclusive, these complement each other.

Ulrich and Smallwood (2011) contended that organizations recognize talent when they realize people are their most important asset. They then start investing on building in-house talents, creating their talent pipeline through succession plans, and fighting with their competitors to grab their talent. While they fight, they lose their talents also. The cycle is unending, the pipeline often gets dried, and the war for talents continues. C-suite leaders in organizations now feel constrained for talents. They spend their time, mandate for more investment in talent development, yet the process never ends.

We are now convinced that top challenge for HR professionals around the globe is talent acquisition and retention. Most of the recent changes in organizational policies, programs, and even in resource allocation, focus on talent acquisition, and retention. For example, grooming talent in-house with knowledge transfer as a policy has been embraced by many organizations. It is not just our succession plan, which restricts our focus on few identified future leaders, for meeting our future top and middle level human resource requirements. Talent management (TM) as an ongoing process encompasses even more. Making the organization talent-driven requires us to institutionalize TM practices. Similarly for acquiring talent, organizations may require to relook into their compensation and benefits programs, performance management systems, knowledge management practices, employee development programs, employee engagement programs, quality of work life, and work life balancing, etc. Again all these are from the point of view of HR management. Talent acquisition and retention even requires many organization level changes. For example, employer branding is a crucial determinant for talent acquisition and retention. HR systems and practices alone cannot be attributed to brand value of organization. Poor customer relationship management, poor after-sales services, poor quality of products/services, organizational structure issues, business performance trends, etc., are also attributable to brand value of organization. For instance, in the recent past, two CEOs or co-CEO model of Wipro complicated the business and the organization structure, resulting talent attrition.

Since McKinsey's seminal research on "War for Talent" (1998), series of researchers focused on the importance of talent to achieve organizational excellence. In a competitive world, when organizational sustainability is an important issue, talent is considered as the crucial determinant (Beechler & Woodward, 2009; Iles, Chuai, & Preece, 2010; Lawler, 2008). Talent differentiates one organization from another. Many researchers (Garrow & Hirsh, 2008; Tansley et al., 2007) believe talent and hence TM are much used and abused terms for lack of clarity on its concepts and constructs.

Such a gap in the concepts and constructs of talent is attributable for its differences in literatures which are mostly consultancy based.

Talent is defined as "systematically developed abilities or skills" of people in organizations (Gagné, 2000). From this generic definition, we come to plethora of definitions on talent. Some of the constructs of talents abstracted from various definitions are:

- Talent demonstrates exceptional ability (Williams, 2000).
- Talent facilitates recurrence of productive thoughts, feeling, or behavior (Buckingham & Vosburgh, 2001).
- Talent amalgamates skills, knowledge, and cognitive ability of employees (Tansley, Harris, Stewart, & Turner, 2006).
- Talent is competence, commitment, and contribution from employees (Ulrich, 2007; Ulrich & Smallwood, 2012).
- Talent is set of competencies required for excellent performance (Cheese, Thomas, & Craig, 2008).
- Talent makes employees exceptional in their skills and abilities (Silzer & Dowell, 2010).

In the above chain of definitions, talent is well perceived as some latent qualities of people in organizations, harnessing which organizations can achieve excellence, differentiating them from their competitors.

So far we have no major dissonance in these definitions. However, the contradictions start when researchers like Stevenson (2010), Stevenson and Lindberg (2010), Adrian-Vallance et al. (2009), Deverson and Kennedy (2005), and Barber (2004), defined talent as natural aptitude or special aptitude, innate ability, personal characteristics of a person, etc. These beliefs *prima facie* make our talent development process redundant. Some of the dimensions of talent that we could understand from various definitions are talent as characteristics of people, talent as natural ability of people, talent as amalgamation of ability, capacity, capability, commitment, contribution, experience, knowledge, performance, potential, patterns of thoughts, feelings or behavior, skills, etc. However, organizations may not always ensure the recruitment of talented people. Hence, for them grooming talent in-house often becomes important.

Acquiring talent through experience is a recognized method, authenticated by researchers like Ericsson, Prietula, and Cokely (2007). From here we see talent from the "mastery" approach, that is, talent acquisition through in-house grooming of people.

This justifies the need of this book to elaborate on professional acquisition, nurturing, developing, and retaining the talent, without, however, demeaning the need for direct talent acquisition through recruitment, wherever possible, knowing well that direct acquisition of talent through recruitment may not be always cost effective, and requires compromising with prevalent systems, policies, and structures of the organization.

The "mastery" approach to talent further extends to "commitment" dimension of talent, which is evident from one's degree of attention and dedication (Pruis, 2011). Employees' commitment is evident from their will, perseverance, motivation, interest, and passion for the job they are doing (Weiss & MacKay, 2009), their willingness to volunteer their energy and efforts for the success of organization (Ulrich, 2007), their decision to continue with the organization.

Final extension to talent approach is considering talent as organizational-fit, that is, the degree of alignment of individual talent with the job and the organization. Here lies the important role of the organization. Through efficient TM, organizations try to enforce the talent-fit.

Your Take—For C-suite

Adding stars to your payroll is not end of talent war?

So you feel you have grabbed the talent and your talent war is over! No. You have to streamline your organization. Did you notice the decay in your organization? Identify it in terms of change in rate of attrition. For every new hire of star talent from competing organization, you create an internal imbalance in the organization. What plan of actions you have to solve this impasse? To overcome this problem, many recommend internal hiring of talent to the extent possible. Does this investment on human capital development streamline your TM function?

Till now, we are centering our discussions on objective connotations of talent or TM in organizations. The subjective approach to talent or TM is more inclusive when it is understood from the employees' and organizational point of view. However, it becomes exclusive when talent is viewed as qualities of some members of the organization, who usually work at the top. Limiting talent or TM only for privileged few may not give enduring results or organizational excellence. For this, organizations require institutionalized TM practices, encompassing all cross-sections of employees.

Final Take

Talent is hardware and software of our mind. Hardware is our acquired knowledge and skills; software is our cognition. Both complement each other.

Organizations create their talent pipeline through succession plans, and fight with their competitors to grab their talent.

TM is an ongoing process encompassing acquisition, retention, and development of talents. Also, it requires supportive compensation and benefits programs, performance management systems, knowledge management practices, employee development programs, employee engagement programs, quality of work life, and work–life balancing, etc.

The generic definition of talent is systematic development of abilities or skills of people in organizations.

Some scholars define talent as natural aptitude or special aptitude, innate ability, personal characteristics of person, etc.

Talent has to be organization-fit, that is, the degree of alignment of individual talent with the job and the organization.

More Critical Thoughts on Talent

Incubate talent in-house! But again there exists the threat, that is, flight of talent. No organization can feel happy contributing to social capital. As do the C-suite leaders! We have many generic approaches to in-house talent development. These can yield results. But we need to be careful, least we do not end up nurturing others' babies.

We are still not clear on what is talent? I have seen companies say that talent is their quality hire, and among those who stay with them for a reasonable period. With quality hire, our talent pursuit is not over. For how long can one retain them is also important. Down to reality, talent means those whose contributions are critical for organizational performance. With talent, people become high performer, and they can churn twice of firm's business than others. Thus talent, at the outset, requires organization to first identify, and then nurture, develop, and retain. The quality of hire has to be assessed using certain metrics. It is always recommended to have cross-functional inputs for the talent metrics. As HR professional we may not understand what talents our materials head requires in a newly hired supply chain executive. Does our materials head expect that a newly hired supply chain executive needs to be more knowledgeable about the market? With such talent a supply chain executive can make the supply chain function more efficient and cost effective. I have seen that a marketing manager assigns more value to those executives who can collect competitors' information accurately and broadly. This is why we recommend that recruitment metrics must encapsulate everybody's requirements. I do not have a quick fix solution for quality hire, but at least I can recommend some action plans that may lead to quality hire.

First characterizes talent in terms of high performer in our organization. What do these people do? List that. Say for example they may be churning "x" quantity of output with "y" defects (say minimum), and "z" revenue level. Consider these points as our benchmarks, and assess the degree of fit of the new hire with such benchmarks.

Repeat such characterizations for every function. With further investigation, translate such characteristics of talent into some measurable criteria, reflecting on observed set of competencies, their attitudes and beliefs, their interpersonal relations, etc. This exercise will streamline our benchmarking criteria, and facilitate in objective assessment of new hire, matching with profile of our organizational talent.

With such reference points, our quality hire for talent becomes easier, as we could make a difference between those who are talented and those who are not. Here, of course, I must sound a word of caution. It is important to assign weights to all differentiating parameters between talented and average people, based on our specific requirement, not just a pleasing personality that may yield high performance of a team leader in a retail mall. I am not saying that he/she has to coerce people to do the work, but at least they must be able to balance the reward and punishment to get the things done.

How did we recruit the talented people earlier? Was it through campus visit, or through some referrals, or from the databases of some manpower vendors? Such reference points may help us in pre-assessing the talent flow. Remember reference points for sourcing talent may be different for different organizations. Indian Institutes of Management (IIMs) and Indian Institutes of Technology (IITs) may not be the only reference points for sourcing top talent for every organization. Larson & Toubro (L&T) could identify engineering talents even from Industrial Training Institutes (ITIs); Microsoft could get CEO from Manipal; a Narayana Murthy of Infosys could come out from University of Mysore. Hence, assess the expectations of our existing talent pool, and accordingly moderate our talent attraction and retention strategies.

Talent is difficult to understand, when the work is assigned in the organizations. We have seen talented people who do not perform. Thus, getting talent is not the answer. Getting and making the talent work, and continue with the organization is our responsibility. This is what the job of TM is. Making the talent work is our responsibility as a manager. See what talent engagement program we have. Do our talented people feel aligned with the organization; are they motivated, loyal to the organization? Ask these questions and find answers. When answers indicate requirement of some workplace adjustment, do so. When it requires change in policies, go ahead with it. Finally when it requires re-crafting our TM strategies, go for it. Remember that talent is situational. When we see an organization is talent-driven, we also assess their work environment, systems, and policies. Those could be our reference points to make our organization talent-driven.

Looking to in-house potentiality for talent is always better. These talents are inexpensive, loyal to the organization, and time-tested. This is why we also require strategies for grooming in-house talent. With our performance management system (PMS), we also track our people's potentiality. If not, we assess from the PMS who are potential talents. However, total weightage on merit-based talent identification through PMS may not be the right answer. Give importance to other parameters like age, qualification, previous experience, cross-functional skills, etc. In this case also we are open to anything that we feel important in the context of our organization. Sense of responsibility and ethical compliances are usually given more weight in talent identification. Nevertheless, after we identify potential in-house talents, we need to strengthen our talent pipeline following some action plans. Such action plans vary with respect to our potential talent matching with hierarchical and functional level. Ulrich and Smallwood (2012) recommended certain action plans for this. For C-suite executives, their recommendation is succession, customization, and modeling. For leadership cadre, they recommend systematic training and development, including long-term training in a leadership academy (when organization does not have one of their own). For high potentials, it is necessary to craft individual development plan. Finally, for employees, it is important to institutionalize talent culture. We have no objection to these recommended lines of actions, but it may not fit with the culture of many organizations, possibly including the one we are anchoring. We have to understand, for most of the organizations—particularly those who have very structured human resource management processes—entry-level recruitment is done for graduates. These new recruits through their process of grooming rise through the levels in organizations. Lateral recruitments are hardly made, unless there is a crisis situation. Thus differentiating from employee development programs, based on their hypothetical distribution to different levels, may create a crisis situation, like the unsatisfied one, who are also talented, may join other organizations. It is hard to say if this could be the reason for Google's executive to join Xiaomi, the Chinese smartphone manufacturer. Google is always hungry for talent. Many acquisitions for Google were for grabbing talented people, rather than adding new value stream to their product portfolio. So when they lose talents, we have the legitimacy to question Google's TM programs. We are also witnessing the reverse talent pipeline syndrome, and the example is Facebook. Reverse talent pipeline syndrome is outflow of our talent, more annoyingly to our competing organizations. Why are talents from Google, Apple, and Yahoo flying to Facebook? Is it because they pay well, provide best work environment, help people in balancing their quality of work life, give opportunity to learn new things, and grow, etc., or is it attributable to their size, now the biggest after acquiring Whatsapp.

Since McKinsey's pioneering research on "War for Talent" in 1998, focus on TM issues have intensified. Human capital management (HCM) or TM, whichever term we use, is now embraced by organizations across the globe. CIPD study (2012), however, could not trace effective TM systems in organization in more than 6 percent cases. Many attribute this to lack of theoretical and empirical knowledge in TM area. Even in our introductory debate, we have struggled to come up with a clear concept of TM, for divergence in its approach. Basic debate on whether talent is innate or acquired (Meyers, vanWoerkom, & Dries, 2013) still remains unresolved. Most scholars agree that talent comprises both innate and acquired components. For this Meyers, vanWoerkom, and Dries recommended use of continuum from "completely innate to completely acquired" to study how TM practices vary across the organizations. In a sense, we are still left to guess what talent is.

Your Take—For C-suite

The war for talent never ends, it intensifies—Are you prepared to fight back?
McKinsey, World at Work, and many others renewed their threat on talent war. If you are not prepared to fight back, you are eliminated from business. To fight back, at the outset, you need to meet the expectations of skilled people. Hence map their expectations first, and understand how far you meet those. If you pay less than

(Box continued)

(Box continued)

market average, then think of pacing your compensation and benefits at market average level. If you spend less than five Mondays in a year for learning and development programs for employees, then make it more, at least 2 percent of annual sales revenue. That makes sense, and people feel that they have opportunity to learn new things and acquire new skills. If you do not have a clearly structured career development programs, then make it clear. Let your people understand the degree of fit of their career goals with the organization. But all these are soft implements of talent war. You can successfully fight back by:

- creating your organizational brand value;
- hiring the right fit (both in terms of individual fit and organizational fit);
- making your presence vibrant in social media:
- investing on human capital development; and
- making extensive use of big data talent analytics, for effective decisions on TM.

Imagining that talent is both innate and acquired, scholars on TM also debated on whether there should be an exclusive approach, or like any other HR function it should also form a part of overall HRM functions. CIPD's study (2012) gives us the answer. Even with global TM wave, only 6 percent organizations have their TM systems. Other organizations have TM, but it is only for the privileged few, say for the C-suite and Leadership roles. More inclusive TM practices are only seen in some organizations, who are not necessarily always IT or technology companies. Whatever may be the stumbling block for TM practices, it is a fact people in TM-inclusive organizations can be excellent performers.

Historically, talent is defined as a unit of weight (Tansley, 2011). Today we define talent as exceptional ability of a person to do something better than others. Exceptional ability or talent of a person combines both innate and learned or acquired attributes. TM as a process first requires the organization to streamline the talent identification system. It may be performance dependent or combination of other factors, such as education, experience, age, competencies, etc. However, operationally organizations are more comfortable with relating talent to performance criteria. Very few organizations relate talent with the employee's degree of suitability with the culture and values of the organizations.

Meyers, vanWoerkom, and Dries (2013) broadly classified literatures on talent into five categories:

- talent as a gift;
- talent as strength;
- talent as (meta-)competencies;
- talent as high potential; and
- talent as high performance.

Although we have arguments and cross-arguments on these literatures, we better avoid such debates, as scholars have grounded talent both to innate and acquired characteristics of a person, which make him/her outstanding in his/her performance over other members of the organizations.

Gallardo-Gallardo, Dries, and Gonzalez-Cruz (2013) suggested conceptualization of talent or TM into object versus subject approaches. Object approaches encompass talent as a natural ability, mastery, commitment, and a degree of fit. Subject approaches acknowledge talent as all people (inclusive) or talent as some people (exclusive).

This book, however, is not intended to debate on TM literatures, rather more focused on TM's value proposition and suggesting the tools and techniques for acquiring and retaining talent.

Final Take

With quality hire, our talent pursuit is not over. For how long we can retain them is also important.

Talent requires organization to first identify, and then nurture, develop, and retain.

It is always recommended to have cross-functional inputs for the talent metrics.

(Box continued)

(Box continued)

It is important to assign weights to all differentiating parameters between talented and average people, based on our specific requirement.

Reference points for sourcing talent may be different for different organizations.

Getting talent is not the answer. Getting and making the talent to work, and continue with the organization is our responsibility for managing talent.

Talent is situational. When we see an organization is talent driven, among others we also assess their work environment, systems, and policies.

In-house talents are inexpensive, loyal to the organization, and time-tested.

Talent comprises both innate and acquired components.

People in TM-inclusive organizations can be excellent performers.

Talent is both innate and acquired characteristics of a person, which make him/her outstanding in his/her performance over other members of the organizations.

Talent Is Human Capital

Acquiring and retaining talent is a strategic imperative for every organization to sustain in competition. Talent acquisition and retention is not just limited to recruitment and motivation. It goes beyond, as organizations have to work out robust strategies for attraction, development, and retention of talented people, even if it requires changes in policies, systems, and structures. It is literal change of perspectives of organizations from human resource to human capital.

Human capital concept per se is a transition from control to commitment approach. Organizations invest in human capital to get incremental change in their business results. Often organizations use the term human capital management interchangeably with TM (Bhattacharyya, 2013). Viewing people as a resource for the organization embeds with our mind-set of exploitation. Contrarily, viewing people as capital legitimizes our investment on people. We exploit resources including human resources to maximize our gains, while we invest in people to build their capabilities to perpetuate our sustenance. However, we have criticism on human capital approach too. People being considered non-expandable asset for the organization, like any other asset, can be owned, bought, sold, or traded. From organizational perspective, when human capital approach is followed, people can be reduced to inert disposable asset when they fail to deliver expected level of performance. Like any other asset human capital value in organization can also appreciate or depreciate. Hence, today people may add value to our business for the talent they posses, but tomorrow they may not, unless we focus on nurturing and developing their talent, and investing in human capital. An inclusive TM approach therefore is better as it is embedded with the culture of the organization, and values the human potentialities, aligning with the business and strategies of the organization.

McKinsey's study is an eye opener for many organizations who still believe in perpetuating traditional human resource management practices, restricting investment on people, and managing them more as a cost to the organization. While human resource cost optimization is important, it cannot be the sole objective of HR professionals for incremental business gains. Thinking long term requires our investment in attracting, developing, and retaining talent, and this can only ensure our sustainability, and prevent our organization from becoming a corporate dinosaur.

While McKinsey's line of recommendations, that is, creation of employee value proposition, long-term recruitment strategy, factoring coaching, mentoring, and experiences to develop in-house talent, and strengthening of talent through investment are understandable, but its implementation requires adherence to rigorous stepped processes for acquisition and retention of talent in organizations. Anchoring the talent pool of our organization first requires us to develop a shared conviction that talent can only ensure our sustainability, strengthening our competitive advantages. Talent is the critical driver of our business. It can propel our journey through uncertainty. Hence investment in talent (both for acquisition and for retention) is legitimate.

Indian organizations, and hence managers and HR professionals, require more cost-effective solutions to TM. Hiring a consultant is cost prohibitive. Moreover Indian business dynamics are different. With maximum population in young age-group, challenge for TM is characteristically different from many industrially advanced countries.

Final Take

Talent acquisition and retention is not just limited to recruitment and motivation. It goes beyond, as organizations have to work out robust strategies for attraction, development, and retention of talented people, even if it requires changes in policies, systems, and structures.

Like any other assets human capital value in organization can also appreciate or depreciate. Hence, today our people may add value to our business for the talent they possess, but tomorrow they may not, unless we focus on nurturing and developing their talent, investing in human capital.

Anchoring the talent pool of our organization first requires us to develop a shared conviction that talent can only ensure our sustainability, strengthening our competitive advantages.

Critical Thoughts on Talent

Originally talent was a unit, either of weight or currency. Over the years it became known as ability (Ross, 2013). Longman Dictionary of Contemporary English, 2006 defined talent as "a natural ability to do something well." This definition reinforces the premise that we all have talent. With this definition, organizations and HR professionals do not have any problem in TM practices, because it can dissuade organizations to refrain from talent differentiation, recognizing equal values for all employees. The problem, however, started when we see differentiation in talent, and compare people in terms of their abilities. Such differentiation persuades organizations to segment their focus on talent, that is, more for those who are highly talented, and less for those who are identified as less talented. Such conceptualization led to exclusive and inclusive approaches to TM. Another possible TM issue, which stemmed from the basic conceptualization of the term "talent," is perhaps our conviction that talent and job success are related. This is also our flawed conceptualization. People with talent by default cannot achieve success, unless they are properly managed. This is why we require effective TM in organizations. An extension of this presumption is our flawed concept that individual success is aligned with the consequent success of the organization. It means when organizations have talented people (who achieve success, as per our earlier assumption), organizations achieve success or desired performance results. Germany's Deutsche Telekom is a good example. The company was full of talented people, despite that it suffered loss, till their ex-CEO Rene Obermann restructured the enterprise, in spite of opposition from the employees. Deutsche Telekom, a company with 230,000 head counts, with business presence in 50 countries, and business revenue of Euro 60 billion is now headed by Tim Höttges.

For such theoretical dilemmas, competency-based approach to talent has been developed. At the outset, this process requires to identify organizational core competencies, and then assess availability of such competencies in employees of the organization. We consider an employee is talented when he/she achieves or performs above average against these core or institutional competencies (Berger & Berger, 2004). In competency-based approach to talent, we also see the conflict between organizational and individual level competencies. Organizational competencies are generic in nature, while individual level competencies are more specific to individual employees. Many scholars argue higher level of performance is attributable to individual level set of competencies (Edenborough & Edenborough, 2012). By that logic talent is identified with individual level set of competencies. To transform an organization to a talent-driven one, with a competency-driven approach, therefore, requires organizations to value core/institutional competencies and individual level set of competencies. This requires understanding of how institutional competencies relate to job specific competencies, or in other words how job specific set of competencies aggregate to institutional competencies. But how can this be done? Let us take a practical example. One of the institutional competencies for a manufacturing organization is "Excellence in Quality." Now for an executive, we can cascade such competency with "quality performance" with some measurable parameters. Does he/she deliver at ±1 percent deviation, which is the permissible tolerance limit on performance in organization? With such approach, to a great extent we can resolve the definitional dilemma of talent or TM.

Another propensity of the practitioners is to generalize talent with the performance and potentiality of the employees. Employees with above average performance are considered as talented, while the rest are not. Along with the PMS, some organizations also put provisions for potentiality measurement. Potentiality assessment helps in understanding the future talents, and accordingly benefits the organization to plan for their development. Succession planning or future leadership roles, etc., is one such example. But employees' performance level widely varies with respect to lot of uncontrollable extraneous factors. Even their potentiality cannot flourish, till the time the right-fit environment comes to surface. Therefore attributing performance and potentiality to employees' talent may not be always correct. Thus developing TM systems based on PMS can only help us partially.

Bell Curve Is Reversal for Talent Attraction and Retention

Bell curve usually known as normal distribution method is used in performance assessment with mandate that only certain percentage of employees (usually 10 percent) would be hyper-performers and eligible for better compensation, learning and development opportunities, and promotion. This class of employees is considered as the talent pool. With their identification, organizations adopt exclusivity in managing talent. Both exclusivity and bell curve are now being questioned in organizations.

First considering handful of employees as hyper-performers, as they perform at exceed expectation level is certainly not a desirable practice. In this process, organizations become more questionable in their TM practices, as many potential talents of the organizations are lost, and they leave their jobs to join the competing organizations. Realizing such potential danger, Microsoft disbanded their forced-ranking (bell curve) method of performance evaluation, and started using statistical models, so that extent and scope of TM practices can cover all cross-sections of employees of the organizations. Similarly, Google has also withdrawn the use of bell curve for performance evaluation. However, Indian IT majors still feel that bell curve is important, as they can easily identify the potential talents, nurture them, and build the talent pipeline for the organization. Indian IT majors believe that the use of bell curve reinforce their commitment to meritocracy. Potential talents of the organizations may not only be those who are hyper-performers. There are many average performers who can emerge as hyper-performers when they are nurtured with some development support. Now imagine a talent-starved organization with bell curve; it may be left with no one who can truly match the company's way of classification of talent.

Some organizations like Mindtree, Mphasis have also discarded use of bell curve in performance evaluation. While Mphasis could replace bell curve with assignment of more weight on individual performance, Mindtree embraced the power-law distribution method which they call a long-tail method to identify hyper, high, and potential performers. Such a system obviously enables organizations to build their talent pipeline with in-house talents, and can ensure better sustainability than their competitors.

As an alternative to bell curve, researchers have recommended some of the methods as under:

- Realistic assessment of various performance groups with a face-to-face calibration approach. This can also help in validating our bell curve-dependent decisions.
- Reinforcing bell-curve results with 360-degree feedback results. 360-degree feedback can also be used as an alternative to bell curve.

- Reintroducing our age-old practice of management-by-objective.
- Introducing peer review.

Facebook: How their PMS contributes to talent acquisition and motivation

For Facebook performance cycle (they call it performance summary cycle) is every six months. Employees of the Facebook, after every six months, collect feedback from their peers (maximum five), assess their managers (to whom they report), and make their self-assessment. Employees then submit it to their managers, who then make performance evaluation and rate the employees. Managers also decide on the prospect of promoting the employees, based on their assessment. System of calibrating such performance evaluation ensures more accuracy and precision, and employees also feel happy for transparency in the performance rating systems. Facebook manages the entire process in two-week time. Although Facebook uses the curve to distribute employees in terms of their performance levels, as per their predetermined guideline, the company claims, it avoids force-choice approach. The curve is rather used to reward the outstanding performers. Obviously Facebook's such transparent performance management approach helps the company to attract talent to the organization, and also to sustain the high motivation level of talented millennium.

Talent and TM are now a strategic challenge for an organization. Globally we see the concerns for the C-suite executives on talent attraction, development, and retention. CEOs of many organizations today allocate considerably time for TM functions.

Some other debates on talent and TM are whether it is innate or acquired. The proponents of innate theories, like Tranckle and Cushion (2006), Gagné (2000), advocated the idea that talent is genetically transmitted attribute of a person, hence it is innate. We can observe early signs of talent in a child and can predict that the child would be talented. However, researchers like Howe, Davidson, and Sloboda (1998) opposed such proposition. More moderate view on talent suggests even if the early syndrome of talent is evident in a child, unless it is properly nurtured through education, training, and mentoring support, the child may not remain talented in his/her adulthood. Hence talent is both innate and acquired.

Without stretching our debate further on what is talent and what is not, let us see the organizational practices on definition of talent and TM. CIPD (2007), based on its assessment of organizational practices on talent and TM, could identify following ideas:

- Talent is creativity.
- Talent is outside the box thinking.
- Talent is drive, energy, applied intelligence, willingness to take on challenges, and the demonstrated ability of the employees to make a distinctive difference to the business.

CIPD's approach to conceptualization of talent, based on organizational practices, does not, however, constraint us to stretch talent or TM debate further. However, we have to draw a line between theories, practices, and operational definitions and connotation of talent and TM. From that perspective, this book explores all possible ramifications of the term talent and TM, before suggesting other important issues on TM.

Organizational effectiveness can be achieved through business aligned human resource management functions, and this can be ensured when organizations embrace TM strategically and holistically. With strategic and holistic focus, organizations can remarkably differentiate them from competitors in terms of effective performance. However, to achieve better results, scholars suggest an inclusive approach to talent and TM functions, so that organizations become truly talent driven, covering all cross-sections of employees under the TM programs. Also, inclusive approach to TM can facilitate in striking strategic balance between employees' performance and potential.

Organization can categorize talent as: C-suite executives and Future business leaders. We have already debated on inclusive and exclusive approaches to talent or TM. Here we do not want to debate which is good or which is bad. For effective TM we need a balanced approach. TM integrates different initiatives, or constructs, into a coherent framework of activity.

Ashton and Morton (2005), while defining TM recommend thinking on the keywords like ethos, focus, positioning, structure, and system. Undoubtedly this approach is more scientific in understanding TM holistically. For example, when we talk on ethos of TM, we mean the underlying values and behavior which are important for a talent mindset. Similarly, according to them, focus indicates understanding of job differences to put the right people in the right job at the right time. Positioning means the commitment from top level management on TM. Structure indicates organizational processes, tools, and techniques required to support TM functions. Finally, system facilitates organizational long-term and holistic approach to TM.

Effective TM requires integration of TM practices with the mainstream activities of the organizations, that is, structuring TM practices as a system of the organizations. With integration as a system, TM functions become more facilitative, and the effect of TM cascades down the organization and make the organization talent driven.

For ensuring integration of TM functions with the organizational systems, Ashton and Morton (2005) also recommended understanding the need, data collection methods, planning, activities involved, and the process of assessing the results. This therefore warns us against blindly copying the TM systems of any organization, hoping its possible replication in other cases. Similarly TM suites now made available by different TM vendors may not be the answer for effective TM practices. We have to test this in the context of our specific organizational needs.

Important conceptual elements of talent and TM

TM is a process of responding to the operating environment through organizational and individual development. Important prerequisites for effective TM in organization are people-focused

(Box continued)

(Box continued)

> work culture. Like Google, we have to recruit people with criti-
> cal skill sets or talents, but at the same time we will also give
> them the free time to pursue their pet projects. As an integrated
> HR management practice, TM helps organizations in achieving
> objectives, like attraction and retention of talents for the right
> jobs at the right time. This is why we also say, TM is conscious
> and deliberate approach both for meeting present and future
> talent needs of the organizations. As an extended approach to
> human capital management function, TM facilitates in recruit-
> ment, assessment, and development of human resources.
>
> TM therefore is a set of practices that are implemented in
> organizations (CIPD, 2011; McDonnell, Lamare, Gunnigle, &
> Lavelle, 2010), and refers to how organizations attract, select,
> develop and manage employees in an integrated and strategic
> way (Scullion & Collings, 2011).

Clarity on Talent Development

Talent development represents an important component of the
overall TM process (Cappelli, 2008; Novations, 2009). Talent
acquisition may be both from the external labor market and from
in-house, through the process of development. In-house talent
development is not only cost effective, being more firm-specific, such talent is more a right-fit for the requirements of the
organizations.

Talent development is one of the core functions of TM, and
today the pursuit of talent development for organizations even
extends beyond national boundaries. Therefore, for organizations,
scope of talent development not just limited within the organization, even the efforts are put to develop talent of associates, collaborators, and vendors, to achieve sustainability and excellence in
performance.

In the pursuit of talent development, organizations again face the
challenges of focusing on generic or specific talent attributes. We
have already suggested that a balanced approach is better. However,

without once again getting immersed with the theoretical arguments and cross-arguments, let us define talent development.

Talent development is a process of planning, selection, and implementation of development strategies for the entire talent pool to ensure that the organization has both the current and future supply of talent to meet strategic objectives, and that development activities are aligned with organizational TM processes. Strategically, organizations adopt unique approach in designing their talent development processes. Such uniqueness helps organization to reduce the flight of talent (as talent is more job and organization specific and not inter-changeable in nature), and enables organization to sustain with their talent in the long run. However, same model may not be followed by every organization.

Managerial Talent

Managerial talents, according to Michaels, Handfield-Jones, and Axelrod (2001), combine strategic mindsets, leadership quality, emotional maturity, communication skills, entrepreneurial instincts, ability to drive business results, and hence the ability to attract and inspire the talented people. A similar notion is proposed by Ready, Conger, and Hill (2010). Based on their contributions, we can list the characteristics of high potentials as follows:

- Consistency in delivering credible strong results.
- Quick mastering of new types of expertise.
- Ability to recognize behavior.
- Propensity to drive for achieving excellence.
- Persistent focus on learning.
- Presence of entrepreneurial spirit.
- Ability to assess risk.

Therefore, talent can be viewed as referring to a limited pool of organizational members who possess unique managerial and leadership competencies. Iles, Chuai, and Preece (2010) have highlighted the lack of consensus concerning which talent may fall within the scope of a talent development process. They emphasized on four possible scenarios: an inclusive approach that focuses on developing each potential employee; an inclusive approach that emphasizes the development of social capital more generally in the organization; an exclusive approach that focuses on developing specific elite individuals; or an exclusive approach that focuses on key positions, roles, and develops talent to fill these roles. The empirical evidence suggests a mixture of approaches in organizations. CIPD (2011) study could also find that many organizations have adopted an exclusive approach that focuses on developing senior managers. There is a lot of focus on high potentials, future stars, future leaders, and high-fliers. However, while the McKinsey Consulting Group initially advocated an exclusive approach to talent development, they now advocate a more inclusive approach that targets development for not just "A players" but also "B players" (Ernst & Young, 2010). Relatively few organizations adopt inclusive approaches. Reilly (2008) suggested that inclusive approaches to talent development are more likely to be found in public sector organizations. Bersin (2010) calls this inclusive approach a form of talent segmentation but with the recognition that all groups of employees have a contribution to make to the organization. Such an approach is consistent with an innovation perspective on talent (Christensen, Johnson, & Horn, 2010). This suggests that all employees should be regarded as great talent given their potential to generate creative ideas. van der Sluis and van de Bunt-Kokhuis (2009) advocated a hybrid approach because it enables organizations to reap the advantages of both approaches, and can keep employees of the organization in general happy and motivated. Ford, Harding, and Stoganova (2010) also suggested that a hybrid approach to talent development may be more appropriate in terms of fairness and employee motivation.

Final Take

Talent is our natural ability to do something well.

In TM practices, the organization has to refrain from talent differentiation, recognizing equal values for all employees.

People with talent by default cannot achieve job success. They need to be properly managed through effective TM practices.

A competency-based approach to TM requires organizations to value core/institutional competencies and individual level set of competencies. This requires understanding of how institutional competencies relate to job-specific competencies, or in other words how job-specific set of competencies aggregate to institutional competencies.

Potentiality assessment helps in understanding the future talents, and accordingly benefits the organization to plan for their development.

Talent is both innate and acquired.

TM is a holistic strategic approach in effective management of human resources. With business alignment, TM also helps in achieving organizational effectiveness.

As a process, TM facilitates in responding to needs to organizational and individual talent development needs, so that with the developed talents, organizations can sustain and grow, successfully responding to the changing environmental complexity. However, this can only be possible when organizations maintain a people-centric work culture.

Effective TM requires integration of TM practices with the mainstream activities of the organizations.

TM involves individual and organizational development in response to a changing and complex operating environment. It includes creation and maintenance of a supportive and people-oriented organization culture.

Talent acquisition may be both from the external labor market, and in-house through the process of development.

Talent development is a process of planning, selection, and implementation of development strategies for the entire talent pool to ensure that the organization has both the current and future supply of talent to meet strategic objectives and that development activities are aligned with organizational TM processes.

Hybrid approach to talent development (both inclusive and exclusive) may be more appropriate in terms of fairness and employee motivation.

Talent Development: Technical or Generic Competencies or Both?

Another debatable issue in talent or TM literatures is what should be the focus of talent development processes? Many organizations struggle to decide on development of technical or generic competencies or both. Traditionally many authors postulated the need for technical competencies with some understanding of the systems and processes to meet the performance standards, including delivering at exceeded expectation level. However, through the process of their grooming, managers acquire generic competencies to rise through the career ladder. Complexities of business today, however, emphasize on balanced mix of both technical and generic competencies. Training is a more effective measure for developing technical competencies, while generic competencies are developed through experiential learning, coaching, and mentoring. Both technical and generic competencies are necessary for talent development.

Generic competencies are problem solving and analytical skills, communication skills, teamwork competencies, and skills to identify access and manage knowledge. Generic competencies also include personal attributes such as imagination, creativity, and intellectual rigor and personal values, such as persistence, integrity, and tolerance (Garavan, Hogan, & Cahir-O'Donnell, 2009; Sandberg, 2000). Generic competencies are contextual. When it is considered in a task context, we consider informational and structural contexts, accountability, and autonomy of the job. In social context, generic competencies require development of interpersonal skills, while in physical context, generic competencies are concerned with issues pertaining to working conditions, like risk, hazard, noise, etc.

In organizations, therefore, focus should be concurrent development of technical and generic competencies, to make available talented people in the talent pipeline, both for the present and future use.

Accelerated or Traditionally Paced Talent Development

This is another important argument for talent and TM. Should the pace of talent development accelerated, or should it be allowed to remain as traditionally paced? A traditionally paced talent development process focuses on classroom lectures, e-learning, on-the-job training, etc. Though time consuming, talent development firmly takes place, enabling organizations to get the flow of talent for long-term sustainability. However, organizations often face the problem of sudden change in competencies, either for new technology, new business process, or new market or environment dynamics. In such cases, traditionally paced talent development process may be time consuming. The compelling need for quick talent development, urges organizations to go for accelerated talent development process. Accelerated talent development programs target for accelerating the learning curve of the most promising talents of the organizations. Here intensive training programs are conducted, using simulation tools, structured projects, etc. Trainers facilitate learning within a short span, so that potential talents can be sent for quick onboarding.

Balancing the traditionally paced and accelerated learning, organizations are now practicing the integrated talent development approach, meeting both the present and future talent requirements of the organizations. This is what Conger (2010) named blended approach to talent development. Conger suggested four components of talent development process, that is, individual skill development, social development interventions, action, and strategic learning initiatives. Blended talent development programs need to be managed through experiential learning (Tansley, Harris, Stewart, & Turner, 2006).

The Architecture of Talent Development

Talent development architecture was pioneered by Gandz (2006). According to Gandz, talent development architecture first requires to espouse a clear statement of talent development needs. Also it should indicate approaches to talent development, supportive HR systems for talent identification, talent assessment, talent development, and strategies for talent development. Lepak and Snell (1999) observed the difference in talent development architecture based on the types of contributions employees make to the business of the organization. For this reason, we cannot have any universal talent development architecture. Understanding of the organization-specific business processes and activities that are necessary for talent development are important to design the appropriate talent development architecture for an organization. Once it is developed, it can standardize and streamline all talent development activities, enabling managers to anchor TM functions efficiently.

Articulation of Talent Needs

From organizational practices, we find that talent needs are interpreted in terms of set of competency requirements. Apart from some generic set of competencies, which are common across all functions, organizations also develop job-specific set of competencies. The process of designing such competencies again varies from organizations to organizations. Through a detailed job analysis, organizations may try to understand the specific job requirements, and the expected level of performance standards. This information they then translate to set of competencies required for the job. Another way could be understanding from the benchmarked positions, that is, through assessment of competencies of similar job positions in competing organizations. Once organizations decide on the job-wise set of competencies requirement, they can integrate it with their performance management systems (PMS), and assess the gap in competencies through performance evaluation. Such gap can be the good indicator of talent needs of the organization.

Another way of assessing the talent needs can be based on the new skill requirement after the transfer of technology, change in business process, and change in market dynamics due to globalization, etc.

All these organizations need to interpret and assess the skill/ knowledge/competency gap, taking stock of existing skill, knowledge, and set of competencies. For example, cross-cultural communication and negotiation became very critical set of competencies for Solvay's executives, particularly after they acquired Rhodia, as their market spread stretched largely to Southeast Asian countries. Such competencies are mostly new, and hence require new talent development initiatives. Many organizations make extensive use of scenario planning to pre-assess the future market and competition dynamics, so that they can prepare them in advance. Such futuristic approach also requires firms to focus on talent development for future jobs. Depending on the changing focus on business and strategies, firms may revisit their talent needs, and meet the talent gap through talent development initiatives. Whatever may be the way for talent needs identification, organizations need to focus on continuous talent development through integrated talent development approach.

Final Take

Complexities of business today emphasize on balanced mix of both technical and generic competencies.

Training is a more effective measure for developing technical competencies, while generic competencies are developed through experiential learning, coaching, and mentoring.

Both technical and generic competencies are necessary for talent development.

Balancing the traditionally paced and accelerated learning, organizations are now practicing the integrated talent development approach, meeting both the present and future talent requirements of the organizations.

Talent development architecture indicates approaches to talent development, supportive HR systems for talent identification, talent assessment, and talent development, and strategies for talent development.

Though appropriate talent needs identification, organizations need to focus on continuous talent development through integrated talent development approach.

TM Practices in Indian Organizations

Indian organizations widely differ in their TM practices. Retaining talent and letting poor performers go is what HCL Technologies follow as their strategy. The company perhaps follows the unique compensation strategies, rewarding top performers more than 100 percent performance bonuses, while de-incentivizing the poor performers. Such exclusivity in TM practices persuades those potential employees, who otherwise could have been the part of company's talent pool of the company, to look for possible opportunities outside the organization.

HCL has ingrained such TM practices to such an extent that top performers, who are obviously the top talents of the organization, expect differentiated rewards, benefits, and career growth opportunities for them. Although the company can retain such top talents to the extent of 90 percent, high attrition of those employees, who perform less, is no doubt a major challenge. This system literally requires company to incur more costs, in terms of replacement recruitment, and induction training. On talent retention, similar exclusivity approach is also evident in case of Tech Mahindra, MTS India, Whirlpool, Dr Reddy's Laboratories, etc.

Abbott India shows tolerance for non-performers, giving such employees opportunities to improve with their 90-day improvement program. With intense coaching, performance monitoring, and feedback, the company could help such potential talents to get back to performance track. Such talent inclusive approach no doubt could make the company more innovative and research driven, to come out with new formulations, maintaining international level quality, and cost efficiency.

Retaining and rewarding critical talent is strategically important for Reliance Communications to sustain in competition. The company believes talent could be the major differentiator for their long-term sustainability. This company also believes that retention of key talent—those who are the strongest performers, have high potential or are in critical roles—is of utmost importance, especially when organizations look forward to capturing aggressive market share. The biggest challenge, therefore, is to devise innovative practices which would disproportionately reward performers, retain them, and help them grow with the organization. Recognizing HR as business partner, the company believes that HR needs to "make things happen" and continuously innovate to stay relevant and offer best solutions in the area of attracting and retaining talent, leadership development, TM, building a performance culture, rewarding high performers disproportionately, and above all driving the right culture and values. Business leaders today expect HR to play the role of an "enabler" for the entire organization and ensure the entire team is focused on a common goal.

Summing Up

This introductory chapter has discussed in detail various connotations on talent and TM issues, within particular emphasis on conceptual clarity and definitions. The chapter has viewed talent and TM as under:

- Talent is hardware and software of our mind. Hardware is our acquired knowledge and skills, software is our cognition. Both complement each other.
- Organizations create their talent pipeline through succession plans, and fight with their competitors to grab their talent.
- TM is an ongoing process encompassing acquisition, retention, and development of talents. Also it requires supportive compensation and benefits programs, performance management systems, knowledge management practices, employee development programs, employee engagement programs, quality of work life and work–life balancing, etc.
- Talent acquisition and retention is not just limited to recruitment and motivation. It goes beyond, as organizations have to work out robust strategies for attraction, development, and retention of talented people, even if it requires changes in policies, systems, and structures.

Managing Talent without Any Barrier— The Cisco Way

With culture of empowerment, engagement, and innovation, Cisco is one of the best talent-driven companies of the world, and even adjudged by many as the best place to work. Being globally dispersed, the company recognizes the importance of cross-cultural values and pursues the diversity inclusion work environment for talent recognition in people from all walks of life. The 1984 company with current head count of 73,834 people, and revenue of US$48.6 billion (2013), emphasizes on number of talent nurturing activities, which also help the employees to feel engaged and maintain their work–life balance. For example, the highly connected workplace of Cisco is so designed that the employees feel the compelling urge to work. Cisco WebEx enables employees to connect with people anywhere in the world at any point of time. Cisco LifeConnections takes care of employees' health and wellness and helps them in nurturing feel-good experience, for security, safety, and general wellbeing.

All the above practices basically support employee engagement, which helps high talent retention for Cisco. With all the above talent nurturing activities for talent retention, Cisco also emphasizes on number of employee development activities. Almost 80 percent of Cisco employees are covered through systematic professional development programs. During the year 2013, the company had invested more than 3 million hours of learning and development for their employees. Diversity inclusive work culture, flexible work environment, and the successive tags of best place to work from different awarding agencies has made Cisco the best place to work today. The company in the process benefits from talent attraction and retention.

Cisco separates transactional functions of HR from TM. Such separation not only makes company's TM functions more and more effective, but also brings their HR functions more proximate to people, resulting an increase in

(Case Study continued)

(Case Study continued)

employees' satisfaction from HR services. Even during recessionary phase, the company has strategically focused on talent development to retain the best performers, sending them all to attend 16-week program with MIT and Stanford faculty members. This clarifies company's long-term focus on talent development.

To strengthen the talent-driven culture, the company embraced the global business services (GBS) approach. GBS primarily focused on shared services and mutual mission, separating tactical and strategic work of HR. Tactical work of HR is more quantitative and operational in nature. But strategic work is more analytic and talent driven. For example, registration and administrative work for training are more tactical in nature, while identification of training needs, designing training programs, ensuring effective training transfer, and training evaluation are strategic in nature.

With integrated GBS, aligning experience and transformation, the company wanted to achieve excellence in HR involving both strategic and tactical issues. As a result, Cisco could effectively manage their talent, sustaining their conventional practices that HR is a strategic business partner of the organizations.

Inputs for this case have been collected from Cisco case study and from the article post of Cisco's HR Head from the following website: http://talentmgt.com/articles/view/divide-and-conquer/print:1

Bibliography

Adrian-Vallance, E., Cleveland, K., Dignen, S., Handorf, S., Hollingworth, L., Manning, E. et al. (Eds). (2009). *Longman dictionary of contemporary English* (5th ed.). Harlow: Pearson Education Limited.

Ashton, C., & Morton, L. (2005). Managing talent for competitive advantage. *Strategic HR Review, 4*, 28–31.

Barber, K. (2004). *The Canadian Oxford dictionary* (2nd ed.). Oxford: Oxford University Press.

Beechler, S., & Woodward, I. C. (2009). The global war for talent. *Journal of International Management, 15*, 273–285.

Berger, L. A., & Berger, D. R. (Eds). (2004). *The talent management handbook.* New York: McGraw-Hill.

Bersin, J. (2010). *High impact talent management: Trends best practices and industry solutions.* Los Angeles, CA: Bersin.

Bhattacharyya, D. K. (2013). *Evidence based strategic human capital management: A study on Durgapur steel plant in strategic approaches for human capital management and development in a turbulent economy.* IGI Global, USA, pp. 53–72,

Buckingham, M., & Vosburgh, R. M. (2001). The 21st century human resources function: It's the talent, stupid! *Human Resource Planning, 24*(4), 17–23.

Cappelli, P. (2008). *Talent on demand: Managing talent in an age of uncertainty.* Boston, MA: Harvard Business Press.

Chartered Institute of Personnel and Development. (2007). *Talent management: strategy, policy, practice.* London: Chartered Institute of Personnel and Development.

Cheese, P., Thomas, R. T., & Craig, E. (2008). *The talent powered organization: Strategies for globalization, talent management and high performance.* London: Kogan Page.

Christensen, C. M., Johnson, C. W., & Horn, M. B. (2010). *Disrupting class, expanded edition: How disruptive innovation will change the way the world learns.* New York: McGraw-Hill.

Chartered Institute of Personnel Development (CIPD). (2007). *Learning and talent development survey.* London: CIPD.

———. (2009). *Learning and development survey.* London: CIPD.

———. (2011). *Learning and talent development survey.* London: CIPD.

———. (2012). *Learning and talent development survey.* London: CIPD.

Conger, J. A. (2010). Developing leadership talent: Delivering on the promise of structured programmes. In R. Sitzer & B. E. Dowell (Eds), *Strategy-driven talent management.* San Francisco, CA: Jossey-Bass, pp. 281–312.

Deverson, T., & Kennedy, G. (Eds). (2005). *The New Zealand Oxford dictionary.* Oxford: Oxford University Press.

Edenborough, R., & Edenborough, M. (2012). *The psychology of talent: Exploring and exploding the myths.* Cambridge, MA: Hofgrefe Publishing.

Ericsson, K. A., Prietula, M. J., & Cokely, E. T. (2007). The making of an expert. *Harvard Business Review, 85*(7/8), 115–121.

Ernst and Young. (2010). *Managing today's global workforce: Evaluating talent management to improve business.* London: Ernst and Young.

Ford, J., Harding, N., & Stoganova, D. (2010). *Talent management & development: An overview of current theory and practice.* Bradford: Bradford Centre for Managerial Excellence, pp. 1–17.

Gagné, F. (2000). Understanding the complete choreography of talent development through DMGT-based analysis. In K. A. Heller, F. J. Monks,

R. F. Subotnik, & R. J. Sternberg (Eds), *International handbook of giftedness and talent*. Oxford: Elsevier Science, pp. 67–79.

Gallardo-Gallardo, E., Dries, N., & Gonzalez-Cruz, T. F. (2013). What is the meaning of "talent" in the world of work? *Human Resource Management Review, 23*, 290–300.

Gandz, J. (2006). Talent development: The architecture of a talent pipeline that works, *Ivey Business School Journal, 70*(3), 1–4.

Garavan, T. N., Hogan, C., & Cahir-O'Donnell, A. (2009). *Developing managers and leaders: Perspectives, debates and practices in Ireland*. Dublin: Gill & Macmillan.

Garavan, T. N. (2012). Global talent management in science-based firms: An exploratory investigation of the pharmaceutical industry during the global downturn. *International Journal of Human Resource Management, 23*(12), 2428–2449.

Garrow, V., & Hirsch, W. (2008). Talent management: Issues of focus and fit. *Public Personnel Management, 37*(4), 389–402.

Howe, M. J. A., Davidson, J. W., & Sloboda, J. A. (1998). Innate talents: Reality or myth? *Behavioral and brain sciences, 21*, 399–442.

Iles, P., Chuai, X., & Preece, D. (2010). Talent management and HRM in multinational companies in Beijing: Definitions, differences and drivers. *Journal of World Business, 45*(2), 179–189.

Lawler, E. E. (2008). *Talent: Making people your competitive advantage*. San Francisco, CA: Jossey-Bass.

Lepak, D. P., & Snell, S. A. (1999). The human resource architecture: Toward a theory of human capital allocation and development. *The Academy of Management Review, 24*(1), 31–48.

Lewis, R. E., & Heckman, R. J. (2006). Talent management: A critical review. *Human Resource Management Review, 16*(2), 139–154.

McDonnell, A., Lamare, R., Gunnigle, P., & Lavelle, J. (2010). Developing tomorrow's leaders: Evidence of global talent management in multinational enterprises. *Journal of World Business, 45*(2), 2–22.

Meyers, M. C., vanWoerkom, M., & Dries, N. (2013). Talent: Innate or acquired? Theoretical considerations and their implications for talent management. *Human Resource Management Review, 23*, 305–321.

Michaels, E., Handfield-Jones, E., & Axelrod, B. (2001). *The war for talent*. Boston, MA: Harvard Business School Press.

Novations. (2009). *Talent development issues study*. Long Island, NY: Novations Group, pp. 1–20.

Pruis, E. (2011). The five key principles for talent development. *Industrial and Commercial Training, 43*(4), 206–216.

Ready, D. A., Conger, J. A., & Hill, L. A. (2010). Are you a high potential? *Harvard Business Review, 88*(6), 78–84.

Reilly, P. (2008). Identifying the right course for talent management. *Public Personnel Management, 37*(4), 381–88.

Ross, S. (2013). How definitions of talent suppress talent management. *Industrial and Commercial Training, 45*(3), 166–70.

Sandberg, J. (2000). Understanding human competence at work: An interpretative approach. *The Academy of Management Journal, 43*(1), 9–25.

Scullion, H., & Collings, D. G. (2011). *Global talent management.* London: Routledge.

Silzer, R. F., & Church, A. H. (2010). Identifying and assessing high potential talent: current organizational practices. In R. Silzer & B. E. Dowell (Eds), *Strategy-driven talent management: A leadership imperative*, San Francisco, CA: Jossey Bass, pp. 213–281.

Silzer, R., & Dowell, B. E. (Eds). (2010). *Strategy-driven talent management: A leadership imperative.* San Francisco, CA: John Wiley & Sons.

Stevenson, A. (Ed.). (2010). *Oxford Dictionary of English* (3rd ed.). Oxford: Oxford University Press.

Stevenson, A., & Lindberg, C. A. (Eds). (2010). *New Oxford American dictionary* (3rd ed.). Oxford: Oxford University Press.

Tranckle, P., & Cushion, C. J. (2006). Rethinking giftedness and talent. *Sport Quest, 58*(2), 265–282.

Tansley, C. (2011). What do we mean by the term "talent" in talent management? *Industrial and Commercial Training, 43*(5), 266–74.

Tansley, C., Harris, L., Stewart, J., & Turner, P. (2006). Talent management: Understanding the dimensions. In CIPD (Ed.), *Change agenda*. London: CIPD, pp. 1–16.

Ulrich, D. (2007). The talent trifecta. *Workforce Management, 86*(15), 32--33.

Ulrich, D., & Smallwood, N. (2011). *What is talent?* Michigan Ross School of Business, Executive White Paper Series. http://michiganross.umich.edu/sites/default/files/uploads/RTIA/pdfs/dulrich_wp_what_is_talent.pdf. Accessed on April 13, 2015.

———. (2012). What is talent? *Leader to Leader, 63*, 55–61.

van der Sluis, L., & van de Bunt-Kokhuis, S. (Eds). (2009). *Competing for talent.* Assen: Van Gorcum, pp. 1–372.

Weiss, A., & Mackay, N. (2007). *The talent advantage: How to attract and retain the best and the brightest.* New York: John Wiley.

Williams, M. (2000). *The war for talent: Getting the best from the best.* London: Chartered Institute of Personnel and Development (CIPD).

2

Attracting the Right Talent

Introduction

Technology companies get talents acquiring failed startups

August 2, 2013, Yahoo bought Rockmelt, a failed startup. Marissa Mayer, the CEO of Yahoo, is in the shopping spree of ailing young tech companies. The purpose is obvious, buy the engineers who built such companies, and lock them with long-term contracts, making such contracts as important terms of reference for acquisition. This is a cheaper option than hiring talents from the market. Yahoo assigns such engineers the job of new product development, and also takes their help in hiring new talents. The extended value chain of talent acquisition for Yahoo, acquiring the failed startups, therefore even stretched to the utilization of social network of such failed entrepreneurs. The process is no doubt innovative and strategically significant for building company's talent pipeline.

However, Yahoo is not the only company in this journey. Apple also often acquires failed startups for getting talents. Apple's acquisition of a failed startup like Color is a good example.

Globally, talent acquisition and retention remain critical issues for many employers. This has been confirmed by series of research studies and reports (Cappelli, 2008; Cheese, 2010; Davenport, Harris, & Shapiro, 2010), carried out by multiple organizations and professional bodies. In fact some of the studies even confirm that talent issues have become top most business challenge. Such shift in organizational priorities from cost reduction to talent acquisition, retention, and development clearly spells out the importance of talent globally. One possible reason is the reversal from global economic recessionary trend, which has increased the global economic activities, and consequent mobility of people, particularly those who are talented. Other reason, of course, is the talent shortage. Over the years organizations, and hence the nation as a whole, hardly put any serious efforts for talent development, resulting a huge talent gap in the labor market.

Renewed organizational focus on talent acquisition and retention, and development, clearly spells out the concern for growth and sustenance, with talent or talented people as key drivers. Obviously for talent shortage, such people are in high demand and find themselves in a better bargaining position than others. Organizations also try to create a win–win situation by paying premium price for the talents. The desperate actions of organizations to acquire and retain talent now even extend to acquiring companies who are already bestowed with talent. Such acquisitions are not for extension of business value chain, but for getting the talented people.

Talent acquisition is an ongoing cycle that aims to attract, find, and select highly talented individuals, based on their potential contribution to the business. It is a hiring process which involves the process of attracting, sourcing, and employing personnel that have the relevant skills and talent in relation to a particular job placement. Putting talented people in the right job helps organizations in achieving their business goals. Scope of talent acquisition now extends to onboarding process of the organization, to ensure new hires are quickly acclimatized with the organization and start delivering results making best use of their talent. For all these activities involved in the process of talent acquisition, it is now managed strategically integrating learning and development, and workforce planning functions of the organizations.

Final Take

Renewed organizational focus on talent acquisition and retention, and development clearly spells out the concern for growth
and sustenance, with talent or talented people as key drivers.
  Talent acquisition now even extends to acquiring companies.
Such acquisitions are not for extension of business value chain,
but for getting the talented people.
  Talent acquisition is an ongoing cycle that aims to attract,
find, and select highly talented individuals.
  Talent acquisition is now managed strategically integrating
learning and development, and workforce planning functions of
the organizations.

Talent Acquisition and Recruiting

For alignment of talent with the business needs, now organizations globally invest considerable time for talent acquisition. Talent
acquisition process is now strategic; therefore, it requires organizations to embrace holistic approach. Holistic approach requires
integration of pre-hire stages of talent acquisition with the entire
life cycles of the talented hires, so that such talent can truly engage
them with the business outcomes. From this perspective we can
distinguish between talent acquisition and recruitment functions
of any organization. Talent acquisition is a strategic approach to
identifying, attracting, and onboarding top talent to efficiently and
effectively meet dynamic business needs. Recruiting is more tactical
and tends to focus mostly on immediate hiring needs. Recruiting
is an element of talent acquisition and includes sourcing, screening, interviewing, assessing, selecting, hiring, and onboarding.
Therefore, recruitment is more a process of filling the open positions. Through the process of recruitment, companies may find
out potential talent in new hires, keeping in view his/her future
utilization in the organization. Therefore talent acquisition does
not necessarily mean only to meet the current requirements.

From different other perspectives also we can differentiate between talent acquisition and recruiting. Recruitment is a linear process, as it emphasizes more on current requirements or needs of the organization. Thus recruitment function is more reactive in nature. In contrast, talent acquisition is a dynamic process and proactive in nature. As talent acquisition cycle is ongoing in nature, among others, it emphasizes on employer branding, employer value proposition, and spreading the organizational information to the target talent segments, to attract them to join the organization. Basically talent acquisition process, apart from actual acquiring of talents, can also create a sustainable talent supply chain. Finally, talent acquisition function is more holistic in nature, while recruitment is a sub-set of talent acquisition.

Final Take

Recruiting is an element of talent acquisition and includes sourcing, screening, interviewing, assessing, selecting, hiring, and onboarding.

Recruitment function is more reactive in nature. In contrast, talent acquisition is a dynamic process and proactive in nature.

Talent acquisition function is more holistic in nature, while recruitment is a subset of talent acquisition.

Steps in Talent Acquisition

Process of talent acquisition follows certain sequence of steps. Here we reiterate that steps are more specific to organizational requirements, as talents are perceived by different organizations differently. Some of the steps discussed here are based on lessons from organizations' talent acquisition process. These are:

- *Documented process of generating lead for potential talents:* Think what would be our technique for lead generation. Nowadays we find many top class organizations are conducting some events related to managerial skill, technical expertise, and innovativeness of campus graduates. For each institution such competition results become a potential talents identification source. Through social media also such events may be conducted to identify talents and then to initiate necessary action to acquire them. For senior level positions, lead generation for potential talents would be through word of mouth, benchmarked information from the competitors, etc.

- *Behavior and organization-fit analysis:* This is a crucial step of talent acquisition. Effective lead generation is not enough. We have to test further the extent of behavior and organization fit of the potential talents. Some behavioral event interview and organization-fit questionnaire are discussed later. Again these are not universal. To the extent possible, organizations must try to test the relevance of these questionnaires in their context, and accordingly bring changes, wherever required. It is important to understand that even when we acquire the talent, we may fail to relate such talent in the context of the organization, as the talented employee behaviorally and culturally may fail to match. Hence, higher the degree of fit, better is the benefit for the organization.

- *Deciding on assessment tools and exercises:* Apart from behavioral event interviews and organization-fit analysis, for culture mapping of the potential talents to assess the degree of fit, organizations also make use of bundle of assessment tools and exercises. We have a number of validated and reliable psychometric tools to test the leadership quality, team building ability, conflict resolution skill, etc. These tests can help us to understand the potential talent. Apart from these, lots of other tools and exercises, like leaderless group discussions, case studies, in-basket exercises, etc., can also help in assessing the potential talent. The underlying idea is to reduce the decisional error in talent acquisition.

- *Reference checking:* Even after successfully complying with all the above steps, to make talent acquisition process foolproof, organizations go for reference checking. Reference checking helps in verification of antecedents of potential talents. Some attributes of potential talents can only be understood when they are in action. Antecedents' verification helps in mapping such attributes of potential talents, and assessing whether these could be deterrents in achieving goals and objectives of organizations.

• *Final selection, onboarding, and integration:* This is the last stage of talent acquisition process. Onboarding process is planned series of engagement for the new hires. Many organizations have their own structured onboarding programs, ranging from three to six months duration. This process involves planning communication and interactive sessions with the new employee periodically, opening up avenues and opportunities for him/her to mix around with different employees. Ideally the company can appoint a guide or mentor to the new employee for the period of six months or more. During onboarding stage HR assesses the views and expectations of new hires.

i.   Induction and orientation stage familiarizes the new hires with the mission, vision, policies, and programs of the organization. It also makes the new employee develop a feeling of being welcomed and "at home."

ii. Integration phase helps the new hires or new talents to get culturally integrated with the organizations. Cultural integration of new talents helps in building their prudence to achieve communication, perception, and cultural congruence.

iii. In many organizations, onboarding, induction and orientation, and integration programs are packaged under their standard induction program.

To grow and compete, organizations worldwide now require talent. Hence, mastering the art of talent acquisition is important. These steps are just helping talent acquisition process, but cannot in any one guarantee our success, unless we are through the entire process of talent management (TM).

Final Take

Talent acquisition follows certain sequence of steps.
Such steps are documented process of generating lead for potential talents, behavior and organization-fit analysis, deciding on assessment tools and exercises, reference checking, final selection, onboarding, and integration. Steps are, however, more specific to organization.

Talent Acquisition Process

Like the steps mentioned above, organizations follow a structured process of talent acquisition. Which process is better, is often learned by the organizations through their practices. For example, many global organizations are now feeling campus hire for talent acquisition is no more a successful process. Furthermore, selecting only top class B-schools or universities and institutes may not guarantee the availability of talents, as talent attributes are even embedded in common or average level intelligent people. Hence, organizations explore multiple processes, and then choose their right method for talent acquisition. In this section, we have elaborated various processes, pacing with organizational practices.

Facebook—The way they acquire talents

Of all the 50 companies acquired by Facebook since 2005, we see the underlying motives are talent acquisition, rather than reaping the benefits of business integration. The company spends millions and millions of US dollars in talent acquisitions using the unconventional route of acquiring companies. However, notable exceptions among these are Instagram, WhatsApp, and Oculus VR.

Instagram, acquired by Facebook in 2012, could benefit in terms of downloading apps and pushing of ads. With WhatsApp in 2014, spending US$16 billion, which is one of the largest

(Box continued)

(Box continued)

> expenditure in the world of corporate acquisition, Facebook could further hit the business of messaging app. Acquisition of Oculus VR again in 2014, Facebook could further integrate the business, extending the Oculus Rift headset to virtual reality space, and thereby creating new business verticals in gaming, communications, media and entertainment, education, etc. The company believes such acquisitions are helping them to extend their multifaceted reach. Other acquisitions, however, help the company to acquire talents.
>
> But why talent acquisition through acquiring of companies, particularly failed startups? For companies like Facebook this is a cheaper option. Such talents can be acquired at competitive compensation and rewards, with long-term agreement to stay.

Analytics or Measures-based Talent Acquisition Process

As strategic significance, and for its ranking among topmost priorities in organizations, decisions on talent acquisition, and consequently TM as a whole, are now increasingly driven by various talent analytics and measures; Globally talent acquisition decisions are now taken leveraging various talent analytics. Based on the employees' data, and benchmarked information from other sources, companies are designing various talent analytics, which are used both for acquiring talent from within (in-house) and from outside. For new talent acquisition from outside the organization, such analytics help in measuring the potential talent of the people, based on which the degree of job-fit and organization-fit can be assessed; ensuring the recruitment is effective, acquired talent can be integrated with the organizational business and strategies. Let us take the example from the corporate world. General Motors, the global giant in car manufacturing, while sourcing the global talent head, emphasized more on the data-driven research bent. Michael Arena, who is now heading the General Motors' Global Talent unit, is a scientist with engineering background. The underlying logic is that Michael would be more competent to take data driven talent acquisition and overall TM decisions. In his own words

Michael said, "HR is being held accountable to deliver business results. And the language of the business is analytics." Other proponents of Talent Analytics, like Mark Endry, CIO of ARCADIS; Ben Waber, author of *People Analytics: How Social Sensing Technology Will Transform Business and What It Tells Us about the Future of Work*, are also emphasizing on data-driven talent acquisition and management decisions.

However, to develop talent analytics, we need to strengthen at the outset our Human Resource Information System (HRIS). With effective HRIS, predictive talent analytics can be designed for holistic TM decisions. Thus, for organizations talent analytics design precedes the foundation level work on HRIS. Initially it is important to capture internal employees' data to prepare talent analytics. With the success of analytics driven in-house TM decisions, benchmarked talent analytics need to be prepared, factoring the competitors' information. With cloud-based technology, an internationally diversified company can synchronize their HR related decisions, and more particularly TM related decisions, based on analytics. Future HR management decisions across the globe for international organizations will be more and more integrated, for effective TM.

After successfully building the foundation of talent analytics through HRIS, next stage of institutionalizing data-driven TM decisions is to standardize a structured approach of interventions. It is important to understand data-driven business decisions, and data driven HR decisions, more particularly decisions on TM issues are not alike. These are different. Even in business decisions using predictive analytics, managers can embrace their specific business intervention. Such intervention may get partially influenced by predictive analytics, and thus cannot be hundred percent structured. Contrarily predictive analytics used for TM decisions need to be structured, to ensure decisional consistency across the organization, even when they are globally dispersed. For example, we want to study the implications of hiring entry-level management graduates and off-hiring some existing managerial employees; with predictive talent analytics we would be able to assess the implications more scientifically, and decide objectively our ratio between new hiring and off-hiring, to balance the human resources in the organization.

Similarly predictive analytics for talent acquisition must also help in tracking employees within the organizations through life cycle. This will help in understanding whether in different stages of career life cycle, employees' performance differs, and when it does, to what extent it can be attributed to their talent. For instance, underperformance at the declining phase of their career is likely due to their outdated skill and knowledge, two important constructs of employees' talent. Organizations may strategically decide whether investing in learning and development for these employees will be cost effective or not. Wherever possible, such employees may be off-hired, or replaced by new talents. But suppose the underperformer is young and had earlier track record of good performance, then it is important to trace the reasons for underperformance. In most cases, such incidents are attributable to discriminatory compensation and benefits design, change of leadership, and partially for composition shift in job skill for new technology or process changes. Whatever may be the case, unless proper tracking system exists, it would be difficult for the HR functions to initiate remedial measures.

Predictive talent analytics help in more transparency in critical HR decisions. This is very important for internal talent acquisition. Once your employees' are convinced that your decisions are objective, their dissension, even in cases where he/she is not considered for a promotion, salary increase, or advancement of knowledge, training, etc., will not exist. Hence, your talent analytics need to be designed in such a way so that it can be transparent enough to reflect the objectivity in decision making.

In addition to above design of predictive talent, analytics requires consideration of other factors like leveraging the complementary skills of IT division of your company, setting up of cross-functional team for finalizing the list of predictive talent analytics, pilot testing the initial group of analytics to study their implications on TM decisions, integrating inputs from external change management experts, etc.

Talent acquisition process of any organization can be facilitated by predictive talent analytics. Talent analytics canvas encompasses all activities of the organization (even beyond HR management functions). Hence, decisions based on predictive talent analytics are more objective, integrated, aligned with business goals of the organization, and finally strategic in nature.

Primarily talent analytics analyze the historical data, interpret those and apply that in real-time basis to assess the implication on talents with respect to shifting business goals and priorities of the organizations. Based on the actual assessment of TM process of organizations, we observe some generic nature of talent analytics, which facilitate in TM, including talent acquisition decisions. Such generic talent analytics are human capital facts, analytical human resources, human–capital investment analysis, workforce forecasts, talent value model, and talent supply chain. Based on the organizational requirements, in each talent analytics suite there may be set of metrics. For example, human capital suite of talent analytics may have employee-level performance data, details on headcount, contract labor, employee turnover, recruitment expenses, etc. Analytic human resources data integrates individual employee level data with the organization, to interpret employee engagement, retention, cost-benefit, HR process, etc. For example, you may decide to make your performance management systems (PMS) more robust, factoring employees' contribution to improve the organizational culture, ethical practices, etc. These you think can give long term sustainability for the organization. Analytic HR data or analytical HR suite can help in this regard. Likewise, each talent analytics suite has its purpose and uses.

Talent analytics at Google

Google through their The People and Innovation Lab (PiLab) designed talent analytics, primarily leveraging their in-house capabilities. Google named is talent pursuit as Project Oxygen. The PiLab, analyzing all HR information of the company could

(Box continued)

(Box continued)

> come out with eight good managerial behavior constructs and five bad managerial behavioral constructs. The pursuit of the company is to develop and promote eight good managerial behavior constructs and to discourage the five bad managerial behavior constructs. This process facilitates in making Google a talent-driven organization.

However, all organizations may not have in-house capabilities like Google to design their own talent analytics. In such cases, organizations may take the help of quality vendors to come out with their own talent analytics, for effective TM (including talent acquisition) decisions.

For C-suite

Your take on big data talent analytics

With IT support HR management functions can churn big data into talent analytics. Talent analytics help in effective TM decisions. For talent acquisition, talent analytics help in framing strategies that can attract new talents to the organization, and also help in developing talents within the organization. In the first case it helps in identifying new hires who are talented and are likely to stay with the organization for a longer duration, justifying therefore investing in building their talents further through sustained investment in human capital. In the second case, that is, developing talents within the organization, talent analytics help in predicting potential talents, based on analysis of present level of high performance, in succession plans, in designing future leadership programs, etc.

However, before jumping on talent analytics, first streamline our human resource management systems (HRMS). Ensure our systems are able to capture data on every aspect of HR function. With this only we can think on big data talent analytics. Next time when we take summer interns from B-Schools assign them the summer internship project on "Big Data Talent Analytics." Gen Y can help, as they are more computer literate and data driven in their decision making. Come out with one or two pre-placement offers (PPOs) for these interns. This will help us in institutionalizing "Big Data Talent Analytics" in our organization.

Final Take

Which talent acquisition process is better can only be learned by the organizations through practices.
Globally talent acquisition decisions are now taken leveraging various talent analytics.
Based on the employees' data, and benchmarked information from other sources, companies are designing various talent analytics, which are used both for acquiring talent from within (in-house) and from outside.
For organizations talent analytics design precedes the foundation level work on human resource information system (HRIS).
Predictive analytics used for TM decisions need to be structured, to ensure decisional consistency across the organization, even when they are globally dispersed.

Creating Talent Dashboard

Dashboard can measure organizational talents and thus can plan for talent acquisition on real-time basis. Dashboard is used with reference to a web-based technology page to collate real-time information on different spheres of organizational activities. The term dashboard is used as a technology-enabled measurement system, as it is intended to track real-time analysis on the performance of organization, more like an automobile dashboard. Automobile dashboard displays the real-time information about the performance of the vehicle.

Essentially, dashboard is a control panel, as it provides graphic presentation of performance information on real-time basis (Bhattacharyya, 2011). How well is the organization doing from the overall perspectives, division perspectives, and department perspectives? Does the organization achieve the performance targets? All these questions can be answered, once the organization is able to design the required dashboard. Therefore, to measure organizational talents, it is possible to use dashboard as a holistic tool.

Nowadays, software vendors make available customized dashboards like Enterprise Resource Planning (ERP) packages. To illustrate, the finance department of any organization can typically use a digital dashboard and scorecard to monitor cash flows, revenues, operating profit, expenses, and other traditional financial metrics. Performance information on a dashboard can appear in a summary form. A digital dashboard can also provide signals in different colors like; red, yellow, or green to indicate degree of achievement of metrics targets. It can facilitate departmental coordination, exchanging performance information, and can therefore promote the culture of teamwork to achieve the results for mutual benefit. For its technological flexibility, it is possible to manipulate real-time information to generate different metric. Depending on the organizational focus, it is possible to shift from one metric to another metric.

Success of dashboards as organizational talent measurement tool largely depends on developing a performance-based culture. People of the organization need to agree in principle on the key performance indicators (KPI) and its measurement through the dashboard.

Digital Dashboards

In many organizations, digital dashboards are used. Digital dashboards provide customized solution for the knowledge workers, making available consolidated information on individual, team, and corporate level, and the external information with the single click of a mouse. Thus, a digital dashboard can function as an analytic and collaborative tool, providing an integrated view to facilitate real-time decision making.

Benefits of a digital dashboard to measure organizational talents can be summarized as follows:

- *It focuses on critical information:* A digital dashboard can reduce the information overload, focusing only on vital business information. Using information filters, it can customize user-specific information, summarize and generate relevant business reports.

- *It integrates information from a variety of sources:* A digital dashboard can integrate information from multiple sources. Key business data, Internet and intranet sites, team folders, and personal files can be organized and viewed easily on a digital dashboard.
- *It fully uses organizational knowledge:* Digital dashboards promote knowledge management culture leveraging each other's knowledge. With the increasing global competitiveness, it is becoming increasingly difficult for people to collaborate with each other. Web-based knowledge management systems better enhance the capability of people gaining access to the best practice views and the underlying knowledge resources.
- *It is a powerful tool for change:* A digital dashboard facilitates organizational change, as people in the organization can use it to read their daily activities, share information, get organizational performance feedback. Such information flow makes people sensitive to the organizational needs of the hour, and makes them feel responsible to deliver their best through self-control.

Final Take

Dashboard can measure organizational talents and so also can plan for talent acquisition on rea- time basis.

Essentially, dashboard is a control panel, as it provides graphic presentation of performance information on real-time basis.

Success of dashboards as organizational talent measurement tool largely depends on developing a performance-based culture. People of the organization need to agree in principle on the KPI and its measurement through the dashboard.

Digital dashboards provide customized solution for the knowledge workers, making available consolidated information on individual, team, and corporate level, and the external information with the single click of a mouse.

A digital dashboard, integrating information from variety of sources can function as analytic and collaborative tool, providing an integrated view to facilitate real-time decision making.

Social Media-based Talent Acquisition Process

Globally companies are extensively using social media, such as LinkedIn, Twitter, Facebook, etc., to acquire talent. In LinkedIn Recruiter, a social networking site, companies can now look for more than a billion profiles and can identify the potential talents from this database. These social networking sites are also enabling companies to acquire talent for their various international work sites also. Some of the important guidelines for sourcing talent through social media are listed below:

- Learn how to properly search LinkedIn.
- Optimize your social profiles to showcase your company and your reputation as a recruiter.
- Learn how to expand your searches—think outside the box when it comes to how potential candidates describe what they do on their social profiles.

Business goals, objectives, and strategies widely vary across the organization and so does their talent acquisition process. However, depending on specific organizational strategies and objectives, effective utilization of social media is possible. Some of the advantages of social media mediated talent acquisition process are tracking passive talents or talented people, who may otherwise be not interested apply for job positions; developing organizational brand value; growing online community; etc.

Leveraging social media, it is possible to strengthen talent acquisition process with some practice-based suggestions as given:

- Install applicant tracking system (ATS) to manage the large database of potential talents for the organizations.
- Make use of public folders for strengthening recruitment database.
- Ensure posting of job openings on social media.
- Ensure usage of psychometric/behavioral tests for job-fit and organization-fit analysis.

- Create a mechanism for immediate feedback after the interview.

Talent Acquisition through Headhunters

Headhunting is a process of profiling the candidates, that is, the potential talents for the organizations. Every organization has their own competitors, where people of similar job profile work. Headhunting process helps in identifying such profiles of the competitors, which can meet the talent needs of your organization. Organization may not be able to go for headhunting. We have professional headhunters available in the market. Headhunting process can benefit organization in getting the right talent.

Employee Referrals for Talent Acquisition

Many organizations promote employee referrals scheme to acquire talents. When talent is acquired through referrals, employees whose reference could make it possible to get the talents are incentivized. For organizations also this process is more cost effective. However, operationally we observe that employee referral scheme is more effective for non-executive job positions.

Talent Acquisition through Employee Value Proposition (EVP)

Organizations struggle to develop their EVP to achieve better results in talent acquisition. In fact EVP can develop and retain talent in the organizations. Many organizations after deciding on their EVP center their talent acquisition decisions revolving on this. For example, any organization undergoing change and transformation needs to increase their EVP acquiring top talents, so that they can successfully manage their change and drive the organization to growth and sustainability. These top talents in the organization would then acquire talents for down-the-line jobs and in the process can make the organization a successful one. Revolving talent acquisition process around EVP therefore benefits the organization and achieves better results through talent engagement. Effective talent acquisition program through EVP makes it more cost effective, as talents can be retained and internally incubated and developed. As a result, dependence on external labor market for sourcing talent gets reduced. With retained talents organization can also increase their value, which in corporate language could be called EVA.

Thus, leveraging talent acquisition process powered by EVP, makes the process more robust, and makes the organization a more compelling place to work for talented people. It facilitates in building the talent acquisition strategies which can benefit both the organization and the talents (both new hires and internal).

Final Take

Social networking sites like LinkedIn, Twitter, Facebook, etc., enable companies to acquire talent.

Social media mediated talent acquisition process can track passive talents or talented people, facilitate in developing brand value, and also in growing online community, who could be the potential talent for the organization in future.

Headhunting also facilitates in potential talents identification.

Some organizations also make use of employee referrals for talent acquisition.

Acquiring top talents, competing with the competitors, organizations create EVP, and then revolve their talent acquisition process around EVP.

Talent Acquisition Strategies

Globally it is well accepted that integration and alignment of talent acquisition strategies are now the topmost priorities of the organization. Most of the organizations are already in this job, but many are yet to consider its importance, presumably for their lack of long-term focus. Matured talent acquisition strategies require adherence to detailed best practices of global organizations, viz., understanding the process of launching a talent acquisition program.

This core understanding helps, as companies can build their strong job profiles, detailing job characteristics, abilities, and qualifications; outlines competently the set of competencies required both for the current and future job; outlines clearly the job deliverables; and describes the recruitment process. Launching a talent acquisition program per se is not a talent acquisition strategy. Understanding it can help in building sustainable talent acquisition strategy.

Like understanding the process of launching the talent acquisition program, it is also important for the organizations to study the process of sourcing, including thoughts on early career program for building talent pipeline, policies on social networking, etc. A particular process of sourcing talent may not be effective with the changing business needs of the organizations. Hence, from time to time organizations need to test the efficacies of the talent sourcing followed by them. Alternative sourcing modes need to be explored whenever required.

Likewise, understanding the process of screening and interviewing talents, process of onboarding, etc., is important to chalk out sustainable talent acquisition strategies. It is advisable to develop the structured guidelines for these two activities.

After basic understanding of the talent acquisition process, and wherever possible documenting the same for the organizations, without however losing the sight of long-term sustainability, before we frame the talent acquisition strategies, it is better to consider following two points:

- *Specific goals and objectives of the organization:* We will certainly not like recruiting top class talent for our routine operation job, say manning a blast furnace using a remote-controlled machine in a steel plant. Contrarily in operation scheduling, in machine design, in supply chain function, we may like to recruit top-class talent. For a certain nature of job, people are available in abundance, while for another, it is not possible. Goals and objectives of the organization keep on changing, and with every change, requirements of talent also change. Thus, the first task in framing talent acquisition strategy is thorough understanding of the goals and objectives of the organizations, and how it affects the talent requirements. In other words, our first talent acquisition strategy should be alignment of the goals and objectives of the organization with talent needs of the organization.

- *Strengths and weaknesses of the organization:* More particularly it is important to understand the strengths and weaknesses of your manpower acquisition process. As a talent manager, we may successfully track talents and interview them, but their onboarding often requires us to obtain approval from the top management, which may take considerable time. In such cases, we may experience a situation that most of our identi-fied talents are reluctant to join our organizations after we get clearance from our top management. In this case as already emphasized strengths and weaknesses need to be understood in the context of our manpower acquisition processes.

Using a detailed checklist, organizations can test the efficacy of their talent acquisition strategy vis-à-vis their competitors. Based on the industry practices, some of the checklists points are listed below:

- Types of human capital investment of the competitors.
- Common identifiable pattern of sources for competitors' talent acquisition.
- Commonalities in job descriptions of competitors.
- Consistency in skill-sets requirements of competitors for sim-ilar positions.
- Performance measurement criteria of competitors.
- Rewards and recognition programs of competitors for talents.
- Career progression path of competitors for talents.
- Use of talent analytics for talent acquisition decisions by the competitors.
- Mechanism for internal talent acquisition.

Let us now understand application of above checklist points, in the context of talent acquisition strategies of a particular organization. Understanding the types of human capital investment of competitors, our organization can frame the strategy on investing in talent. Many organizations focus on firm-specific investment on talent, rather than general talent development. In case of general talent development, firms often face the problem of losing talents to competitors. Focusing on firm-specific talent development is also more rational, as it can help in accurate measuring of return on investment on talent or human capital. We have a long stretch of debate on right or wrong of both these approaches. We are not asking to ape our competitors, we are suggesting at least to draw lessons from our competitors' practices, and then decide our strategy. In fact this can appropriately make our strategies more robust, ground-tested, and result oriented.

Similar understanding of the common identifiable pattern of sources for competitors' talent acquisition, ease the process of our strategy selection. Likewise information on degree of commonalities in job descriptions, consistency in skill-sets requirements, performance measurement criteria, rewards and recognition programs, career progression path, use of talent analytics, and mechanism of talent acquisition, etc., can at least help in rationalizing your strategies for talent acquisition.

Globally organizations are trying to leverage their talent acquisition strategies for gaining competitive advantages. For developing talent acquisition strategies, at the outset organizations follow the mentioned guidelines, assess their position vis-à-vis their competitors, using the recommended checklists, and then finally come out with their strategies to create distinct competitive advantages over others. Success of talent acquisition strategies largely depends on employer brand, appropriate targeting of the talent pool, selecting the right process.

Successes of talent acquisition strategies also depend on selection of the appropriate technology enabled talent-suite by the organizations. Even though we have already delineated the processes and steps, with the increase in the complexity of TM function and its strategic importance for business growth and sustenance, organizations today prefer technology enabled talent-suite. Such talent-suite can integrate the entire TM processes, and thereby facilitate effective decision making in talent acquisition. A good talent-suite can provide an integrated platform to analyze performance of individual employees, and how such performance could help in achieving the business results of the company. Also talent-suite can assess how the competencies of the employees are matching with the organizational needs, potentialities of employees, alignment of the talent acquisition with the succession planning, entry level hiring, and the process of onboarding. For such integration, using talent-suite, managers can also generate various talent analytics, which can benefit in framing future talent strategies.

Finally along with the framing of strategies, it is also important to focus on organizational brand building and making employees brand ambassadors, creating a workplace which provides opportunities to experience something better and feel good and engaged, strengthen the social network of the organization, focus on hiring for the culture-fit, focus on big data analysis, etc.

Your Take—C-suite

What you do in building a robust talent strategy?

You know talent now plays important role in your organizational success. Hence, it is now important for you to build a robust talent strategy. But the question remains how? Try these quick-fix solutions for results.

Be proactive in framing talent strategies—this requires you to spontaneously initiate those actions which can promote employee engagement, retention, recognition, and investment in human capital development.

Align your talent strategies to business goals and organizational strategies.

Make extensive use of big data analytics in framing your talent strategies.

Top Strategies for Talent Acquisition

In a competitive market for talent acquisition, organizations are always innovating in their own strategies to get edge over their competitors. I have seen many entrepreneurs, knowing well that they cannot acquire the talent, competing against large organizations, make effective use of relationship with potential talents. Many family managed business units in India still attract talent through such relationships. On acquiring new talents, such organizations plan for new business expansion. This is just opposite in large corporatized organizations. Usually in large corporatized organizations, talent acquisition process precedes business plans and new strategies for development. However, there are also exceptions. We have many large corporatized organizations, whose talent acquisition process is ongoing, irrespective of hiring needs. Such organizations obviously succeed in institutionalizing TM functions.

Emulating the talent acquisition strategies from best practices of organizations spread across the globe, we find how companies differentiate their talent acquisition strategies. Technology-enabled talent tracking process identifies talent through social media. Organizations build relationship with such prospective talents, and finally succeed in the process of acquisition. Strategic talent acquisition combines firm's strategies, capabilities, and technologies. Building a talent pipeline for online talent communities is a new strategic move for talent acquisition, as it can help organizations to build a strong database for talent to meet their present and future talent requirements. Instead of sending just job alerts to this talent community, it is desirable to focus on organizational branding, participating in discussions, sharing information, intellectual exchanges, etc. Positioning organizations in knowledge sharing communities gradually transcends the talent in nurturing positive attitudes toward the company, and at opportune moment they also feel like attaching with such organizations.

Hence, new talent acquisition strategies for organizations focus more on branding through social media, and meticulously exchanging information, sharing knowledge, and leaving a lasting impression about your organizational values. Other new talent acquisition strategies are diversity neutral recruitment, increased focus on incubating in-house talents, more differential weights on job experience.

Talent acquisition strategies for Google and Yahoo are funda-mentally different. Yahoo believes in "talent scarcity hiring pro-cess." Yahoo feels this ensures best talent acquisition. Contrarily Google believes in not "weeding out the weak." Experts say Yahoo's talent acquisition is a "catch-22" situation, as the com-pany believes in hiring the best talent from who applies. Yahoo's recent two dozen acquisitions in 17 months timeframe are more for scouting talent than anything else. But the question remains who can shop with Yahoo for talent like this?

Final Take

Integration and alignment of talent acquisition strategies require adherence to detailed best practices of global organizations, and understanding the process of launching a talent acquisition program.

It is also important for the organizations to study the pro-cess of sourcing, including thoughts on early career program for building talent pipeline, policies on social networking, etc.

Similar understanding of the process of screening and inter-viewing talents, process of onboarding, etc., are important to chalk out sustainable talent acquisition strategies.

To frame effective talent acquisition strategies, we need to understand specific goals and objectives of the organization, and also the strengths and weaknesses of the organization.

A detailed checklist to test the efficacy of the talent acquisi-tion strategy can help immensely.

Also, the success of talent acquisition strategies largely depends on the selection of appropriate technology enabled talent-suite by the organizations.

Along with the developing of talent acquisition strategies, organizations need to focus on brand-building.

Building relationships with potential talents through social media is a strategic talent acquisition process.

Strategic talent acquisition combines firm's strategies, capabilities, and technologies.

Talent acquisition of 3M

For 3M, talent is an inclusive term, and so is TM. The century-old organization progressed over the years, delivering innovative products, for the contribution of employees, which the company widely acknowledges. "We are successful because we work together ... and every team member is a leading contributor." The company is among top ten best companies of the world in terms of talent acquisition and retention. In addition to the best TM practices to retain their brand value as the best company to work, 3M makes use of their best strategies to focus on in-house talent development, like creating opportunities for the professionals in different verticals of their choice.

Thus, unlike Facebook, 3M believes in talent acquisition, attracting talents, creating their brand value, that is, best place to work, and focusing on continuous talent developing, so that present employees can be future ready for leadership roles.

Ethical Issues in Talent Acquisition

To begin with, let us understand values and ethics at the outset. Values are our deeply held beliefs, and ethics are moral rights and duties. For organizations, values may not be always documented, but ethics in the form of guidelines may be there. Both values and ethics influence our decision making. In talent acquisition, ethical issues are mostly visible in recruitment and selection process. We have already stated that recruitment and selection is a subset of talent acquisition. To attract talent, organizations often share information with the target new-hires, which are far from the truth. A new-hire may not have the total picture about the organization he/she is joining. Hence, their decision to join the organization substantially gets influenced by the information they receive from the organization, in the process of their selection. This is a gross ethical violation. While interviewing the target talents, organization often tries to extract confidential information about their current place of work.

For organizations, ethical concerns in talent acquisition develop only when they value it. As we do not have any legal restrictions, in one way or the other, organizations try to violate ethical issues, partly for their ignorance, and partly for the absence of any structured guidelines. However, organizations which follow in general good governance practices and which have encapsulated values and ethics with their business practices comply with ethical issues in talent acquisition also.

In the absence of structured ethical guidelines for talent acquisition, to ensure ethical compliance, organizations always insist on adherence to the legal provisions, if any, urge for testing the merit of the decisions putting the decision makers in the role of stakeholders, etc.

Final Take

Both values and ethics influence our decision making. In talent acquisition, ethical issues are mostly visible in recruitment and selection process.

For organizations, ethical concerns in talent acquisition develop only when they value it. As we do not have any legal restrictions, in one way or the other, organizations try to violate ethical issues, partly for their ignorance, and partly for the absence of any structured guidelines. However, organizations which follow in general good governance practices, and which have encapsulated values and ethics with their business practices, comply with ethical issues in talent acquisition also.

In absence of structured ethical guidelines for talent acquisition, to ensure ethical compliance, organizations always insist on adherence to the legal provisions, if any, or consider the merit of the decisions from stakeholders' perspectives.

Acquiring Talent in a Talent-driven Market

With globalization, job mobility and access to information have now increased considerably, resulting increase in bargaining power of talented people. Today people with talent can dictate their terms. They are choosy in selecting their place of work. They have control over their careers. Obviously all these reasons have now made talent acquisition process more and more competitive. To achieve success in such a competitive market for talents, companies are now more innovative and strategic in their talent acquisition. Some of the important steps for talent acquisition in a talent driven market can be listed as under:

- Strengthen TM function by building in-house capabilities or partnering with reputed talent advisory services. Building in-house capabilities may not be immediately possible as it requires not only sustained investment, but also gaining experiences to make TM function more and more time tested. Hence, for getting immediate results in talent acquisition in a talent-driven market, it may be prudent to partner with some trusted talent advisory firms.
- Continuously audit and monitor talent needs to understand the short- and long-term talent requirements of our organization. It requires strengthening internal TM function with provision for both in-house and external audit. Such audit and monitoring can help in identifying talent gaps, understanding critical shortage of skill and competencies set, and accordingly signal organization to prepare for appropriate talent acquisition process.
- Prepare talent acquisition strategy. Talent acquisition strategy needs to be prepared in alignment with the business strategy of the organization. With absolute sync companies can decide their action plans in talent acquisition well in advance than their competitors. It is important to prepare the talent acquisition strategy with a long-term focus, referring to the long-term business strategy of the organization. A well prepared talent acquisition strategy can also outline the process of talent acquisition both in-house and externally.
- Ensure acquired talents are taken through onboarding process of the organization, and give them a feel-good experience. Onboarding program has to be designed and operationalized in such a way that new hires find their workplace better

than their earlier one, they can feel ease to integrate with the organization quickly, etc.

- Finally, also remain dedicated to talent even in a passive market situation. Many organizations even risk losing their talents in a situation of market downturn. Some may even deliberately lose talent for sustaining through cost savings. But such strategies need to be weighed in terms on long-term results. With business boom, needs for talent may again emerge, and at that point of time, organizations may face the difficulty to acquire them.

Keeping these points in mind, organizations may draw their talent acquisition programs. Such programs may be to use employee referrals scheme, social media, selective use of headhunters, professional services, etc.

Final Take

In this competitive market for talent, TM function of any organization has to build in-house capabilities, partnering with talent advisory services.

It also requires continuous audit and monitoring of talent needs, developing talent acquisition strategies, taking acquired talents through the onboarding process, and also continues with the talent acquisition pursuit, even when the market is dull.

Apart from professional services of talent advisory firms, companies can also make use of employee referrals scheme, social media, and selectively the services of headhunters.

Attracting, Acquiring, and Motivating Millennial Talents

To attract and motivate millennial talents with pay is now becoming an outdated approach, though we cannot state it emphatically in absence of adequate empirical data. Companies are trying to be more and more digital, tech-savvy, and innovative for the millennial talents. The new business models encompassing the digital age now require companies to be more alert in TM practices, more flexible to accommodate the changing expectations of millennial and the new generation of customers.

The psyche of millennial, as observed in the organizations by researchers, is to discard job which is inflexible, and also to dislike a manager who still believes in inflexibility. They want to be more empowered. It is also important for companies to learn from the millennial, rather than treating them as unmanageable. Manage them with some compelling mission, so that they legitimize their purpose of doing the job. Also design the job accomplishing which they get a sense of pride, and feel that they could genuinely accomplish something new, challenging, etc. Some of the other expectations of the millennial evident from several research reports are strong desire for stability, companies which value new ideas, and innovation.

For GE millennial talents get attracted for a purpose

For GE, attracting and retaining millennial talents is obviously a great challenge. GE believes in not just imagining, but doing. With a culture of opening innovation, this century-old company today provides world class manufacturing and processes solutions. GE's open innovation is powered by open collaboration. Experimenting, collaborating, and learning are the three important areas through which GE continues unceasingly to attract the millennial talents across the world. GE proclaims it is a company of ideas. For GE culture is contextual. Like reengineering of business portfolio, operation processes, the company also reengineers their culture, to pace with the changing mindsets of the young generation, so that they find the company as their preferred destination for self-development, earning, and learning.

With a promise to millennial talents that the company believes in a purpose, GE today is successful in attracting, motivating, and retaining millennial talents.

Millennial talents can be motivated and retained when the organizations understand them, map their expectations and become flexible to design their compensation package. Understanding millennial is possible when organizations make use of analytics and metrics, and psychometric tools, to assess their fit with the job and the organizations. Matching compensation with millennial talents requires understanding their needs. Millennial may not be interested in deferred benefits; they want more cash in hand now. Also millennial expect their employers to be more inclusive in diversity issues, and sensitive to the employees' need for work–life balancing. They expect their organizations to provide them opportunity to grow at quick succession, more functional autonomy, more opportunity to learn, and of course a sense of purpose to justify why they work for the organization. And even with all these, organizations also need to prepare for their problem of attrition. Hence, motivating millennial talents requires series of strategic and sustainable HR management practices.

Challenges in Talent Acquisition

Talent acquisition is now one of the most important challenges of the organization. This has now been confirmed by a series of studies by many top class global consulting organizations. Some of these studies on talent acquisition issues emphasized on the need for internal grooming of talent, strengthening their succession planning, and promotion-from-within policies. Particularly, the global trend of grooming C-suite managerial employees within the organizations, launching of future leadership programs by organizations, etc., are some of the important indicators for talent incubation within the organizations, so that future talent crunch can be avoided. But every organization may not be privileged with the talented people, or potentially talented people. Organizational talent pipeline may not be well developed or totally dried up for absence of potential people within the system. In such cases however, organizations need to emphasize on acquiring talent from external sources. Since talent acquisition is relatively a recent approach, whatever literature supports we get are from corporate practices. Thoughtful organizations and leaders build strategy around acquiring talent to meet both current and future business needs. Before adding staff or simply filling a vacant position, it is important to have clear sense of the talent gaps as they relate to the skill sets needed to meet current and future performance requirements. Otherwise, we are simply adding people that may or may not contribute to the organization's success.

Having a clear sense of the strengths, weaknesses, and opportunities within teams/work groups allows managers to make a more calculated decision about their next hire. For example, if our market and customers are demanding a more sophisticated product or service, you may need to adjust our recruitment and sourcing strategy to hire a more specific, technical skill set. HR functions can assist business leaders with workforce planning to assess the supply, demand, and gaps existing between currently available and needed skill sets required to deliver on the business plan.

Once a gap analysis has been conducted and managers have a good sense of their staffing needs including the availability of talent, they are in a position to execute a plan to acquire the needed skills and talent. Often organizations will use more than one method (e.g., recruiting, sourcing, training, and development).

Creating Employment Brand

Going to market for talent is like going to market to sell products and services of companies. Each organization has a unique culture, which comprises set of values, beliefs, attitudes, and behaviors shared by the employees. It's the way people interact with each other, the way they go about work and the practices of the work environment. Building a solid, positive organizational culture is critical to gaining competitive edge and reaping the benefits of loyal employees, which in turn provides increased profitability.

The first step in creating or changing culture is to define it—identify what makes company unique. An employment brand is an internalized sum of images and impressions a company makes on an individual. Organization through the process of its work sends a message. These messages when interpreted by people positively, help in creating a brand value. When such brand value can create a compelling image, people with talent want to join and continue to work with the organizations.

A few recommended action plans for creating an employment brand value are:

- Assess existing culture and value proposition.
- Find out gaps, if any between what organizations actually promises and what organizations achieve.
- Identify our advantages vis-à-vis our competitors.
- Review what we offer to new talents as an employer.
- Identify what we resolute as our values.

After the successful process of creation of employment brand, companies develop their brand statement, to reflect on the type of values and culture they espouse. Such brand statement articulates unique value proposition for the targeted talents, which makes a compelling pressure to join the organization. For example, a tagline with employment advertisement, like "Innovators and Advocates of Change" reflects the brand value of the organization. In the workplace of such organization, people with talent can get their desired platform to pursue their innovative ideas and function accordingly.

A quick-fix solution for creating an employment brand is to take steps in building a platform or hub making use of Facebook or LinkedIn. This platform would facilitate exchange of thoughts between current employees, past employees, and prospective applicants or talents for the organization. Interactions will increase the flow of thoughts and in the process help in branding the organization. Just by creating a platform is not enough, organization also needs to spread the word of mouth, so that people feel interested to join the interactions and contribute. This requires from the organization part also being more transparent about information sharing, tolerance for criticism, integrating the interaction results with the organizational change, etc. With all these the talent community for the organization is created, which will also improve the organization capabilities for talent acquisition.

Talent Organization-fit and Job-fit Analysis

Every organization has its unique culture. In talent acquisition, it is important to assess whether the new-hires match with the culture of the organization, that is, how far their values are compatible with the culture of the organization. This organization-fit analysis is simultaneously done by the organization and also by the new-hires, so that mutual compatibility is achieved for a win-win result. Let us discuss this issue in the context of organization. A particular organization's culture is highly focused on customer services, obviously this organization will expect in their talents also reflection of similar culture. Hence during the selection process, such cultural constructs, that is, believing in customer services will be verified by the organization, administering different tests, such as use of questionnaire, personality assessment, in-basket exercises, role plays, etc. With high degree of match, it becomes mutually satisfying.

In case of job-fit analysis, contrarily in talent acquisition, competency-based assessment helps. Along with culture or organization-fit analysis when the job–fit analysis results are combined, organizations can not only hire the right talent, but can also ensure retention of these new hires for their compatibility. Previous job analysis and design of structured job descriptions help the organization to map the talent requirements for specific job positions. For instance, if a particular job position requires presence of following attributes in a newly hired talent: collaboration, teamwork, adaptability, patience, and multitasking. To measure how far such elements are present in the potential talented employees, test measures are administered in the selection process, including interviewing of the candidates. Apart from structured psychometric tests, interviews are more effective measures, as at this stage only it is possible to assess the desires and motivational fit of the new talents or new hires in the organization.

Nature of talent widely varies with respect to the job positions. For example, in a sales job, which is more commission-based than fixed earnings, companies may not insist on customer relationships management (CRM) or long-term customer relationships.

Hence, nature of talent in such job positions may stress more on those qualities which can convince people and persuade them to buy. Contrarily for a sales profile, for which fixed income earnings are more emphasized than commission, CRM and long-term customer relationship would be considered more important. Hence depending on job position and organizational internal value percepts on jobs, talent requirements may widely vary.

Finally, job-fit and organization-fit analysis only cannot yield better talent acquisition decisions. New hires need to have adequate capabilities to perform his/her job roles successfully. In the interview process, this aspect is also cross-checked, so that new hires are more productive.

Final Take

Thoughtful organizations and leaders build strategy around acquiring talent to meet both current and future business needs.

Before adding staff or simply filling a vacant position, it is important to have a clear sense of the talent gaps as they relate to the skill sets needed to meet current and future performance requirements.

Going to market for talent is like going to market to sell products and services of companies.

Building a solid, positive organizational culture is critical to gaining competitive edge and reaping the benefits of loyal employees.

Organizational brand value can be created by assessing the existing culture and value proposition finding out gaps, our advantages against the competitors, and finally what we resolute as our values.

A quick-fix solution for creating an employment brand is to take steps in building a platform or hub making use of Facebook or LinkedIn.

In talent acquisition, it is important to assess whether the new hires are matching with the culture of the organization, administering different tests, like use of questionnaire, personality assessment, in-basket exercises, role plays, etc.

Similarly job-fit analysis is done using competency-based approach.

Organization-fit and job-fit analysis when done for talent acquisition, it can not only ensure right talent, but also retention of new hires for their compatibility.

Talent Acquisition—Decision-making Dilemma

For talent acquisition, HR departments are faced with two types of decision-making dilemma—content-based decision-making systems and process-based decision-making systems. Content-based decision challenges are rooted in making quality decisions based on accurate information, data, and corporate support. They are embedded in quality, accuracy, and precision. Process-based decision challenges revolve around the structure of decision making, involvement of stakeholders, as well as efficiency and timeliness of decision making. In most organizations, the talent acquisition function is still not used to assist in the development of corporate strategy, at least not in any real way. As a result, HR department is not formally invited to participate in the formulation of corporate strategy. Irrespective of the fact whether HR department is invited or not, they can contribute to this phase by aligning corporate strategy with their tactical and transactional activities. The influence should arise from the interpretation of corporate strategy, as well as influencing key stakeholders. Holistic approach to talent acquisition strategy encompasses all the tools, practices, and systems that will be used to achieve organizational objectives. Aggregation of all these methods to accomplish the goals of the organization is what we call strategy.

In framing talent acquisition strategies, following issues need consideration.

- Does your talent acquisition strategy help in achieving mission of your department/division?
- How far does your talent acquisition goals affect overall organizational goals?
- Does the timeframe for achieving the overall strategic intents match with your individual or departmental time frame?
- What would be the learning curve effect for the newly acquired talents? Will such effect be a deterrent in achieving intents of our talent acquisition?
- What would be the adverse effect in case your HR department fails to acquire talent?

By answering these questions, you can make talent acquisition strategies more meaningful. Process and content decision-making systems establish the link between strategy and tactics. Well-designed decision processes in talent acquisition are efficient, participative, and inclusive. Similarly well-designed decision content provides a high quality of information to the HR management functions, and also stimulates support from the stakeholders of the organizations.

Final Take

Talent acquisition faces two types of challenges—process-based decisional dilemma and content-based decisional dilemma.

Process-based decisional challenges revolve around the structure of talent acquisition decision making. Content-based decisional challenges are rooted in making quality decisions based on accurate information, data, and corporate support.

Holistic approach to talent acquisition strategy encompasses all the tools, practices, and systems that can be used to achieve organizational objectives. Aggregation of all these methods to accomplish the goals of the organization is what we call strategy.

Talents, Managerial Skills, and Competencies

In this section we are trying to understand talents as integration of skills and competencies. Skill is some goal-oriented learned or acquired actions to perform a task. For every job in the organization, some specific skill sets are essential. From operations management point of view, we can divide skill in to two types—overt responses and controlled stimulation. Verbal, motor, or perceptual types of skill sets are categorized under overt responses. Verbal skills are speaking, which is important to maintain interpersonal relations. Motor skills are appropriate movements of limbs and body, particularly important as operating at shop floor level. Perceptual skill understands sensory responses. Like skills for the overt responses, for controlled stimulation, we require skills in the form of energy inputs. With technological changes skill requirements alter, as do the requirements of the talent profile.

Technological changes per se require broader variety of skills and higher average skills from the workers. From another viewpoint, technology is instrumental in fractionating and de-skilling of jobs. Technological change not only redesigns the job, but also alters the skill, knowledge, and competencies requirement, requiring new talents in the organizations. For example, in India structural change in the occupational pattern is evident from 1981 census onward. Requirements of manual or blue-collar workers have now significantly reduced, while more white-collar jobs are now created. Some white-collar jobs are even highly knowledge-intensive. Such compositional shift in the skill requirements gradually increased the demand for talent in organizations, as today's jobs are not only characteristically different, but also critical in nature. Greater level of technological literary, even for lower skill and low paying occupations will be in demand in future. Thus, in the era of technological change and globalization, through skill change or upgrade, organization can also achieve effectiveness and excellence, acquiring talents.

Based on these discussions, we can understand the process of change in the organizational talent profile with the technology or process-induced changes. Today we are more comfortable in using the term "talents," instead of skills, knowledge, and even competencies. However, core concept of skill cannot be neglected, as the base of talents today lies in the skill sets of the people working with the organizations. Like categorization of skills into technical, supervisory, interpersonal, and general business types, we can only think of talents in terms of generic and technical. This we have already discussed in Chapter 1 in detail.

For talent acquisition and talent acquisition planning, organizations need to design skill inventories with detailing of the information on the employees, their job-related skills, training, and/or experience that can benefit organization in future job allocation and assignment, etc. Although conventionally we use skill inventories in organizations for quick identification of right person for effecting promotion and transfer, for TM we use it more as talent pipelines, for meeting the current and future flow of talents in the organization.

Let us assume our organization is now planning for global expansion. A well-documented skill inventory can quickly identify availability of those employees with required talents from the database of the organization and select the suitable candidate for the job. Thus, maintaining a skill inventory is essential for effectively managing the talent in organization also.

Multi-skilling

For developing in-house talents, multi-skilling of employees is very important. Multi-skilling is training employees on different skill sets, so that they can be used for multitasking. Multi-skilling also emphasizes on developing cross-functional skills through cross-training, so that employees can develop their holistic talent, making effective use of their full potentialities. Complexities of business process now emphasize on multi-skilling. People with multiple skill sets become more talented, and this is why we say multi-skilling changes the talent-mix, and enhances the competitive strength of the organization.

Talents and Skills for the New Millennium

In the changed global business scenario, organizations need to develop following talents and skills in all cross-sections of employees to sustain in competition, and to achieve excellence.

- *Partnerships and collaborations skills:* In the new millennium, managerial talents across all levels need to understand the importance of strategic associations. It is such a critical skill set, without mastering it, managers would not be able to identify partnership and collaboration opportunities, understand the structure of working relationships with the partners or collaborators, or negotiate the terms and close such deals. Both at the national and international levels, organizations are forging strategic alliance to strengthen their market position. Even in terms of domain of market, two companies can have alliance of no-competition. For example, to reduce the rate of attrition, IT companies have made no-poaching agreement with each other. Partnership and collaboration skills require managers to continuously scan the environment and identify such opportunities to achieve the strategic objectives.

- *Quick decision-making skill:* Developing skills for quick decision making is also very important. Delaying response time to change will lead to the loss of market opportunities. Hence, managers need to master the art of quick decision making, developing their capability to understand the change scenarios. Managers need to understand that monitoring day-to-day operations is one aspect, and making a strategic move in the changed situation through quick decision making is another aspect. In a dynamic business environment, many organizations ensure quick decision making or response, pre-conceiving the scenarios and structuring the strategies, so that in a given scenario, they can quickly take the desired decision. However, such decisions need not always be error free. Even then it benefits the organization as early mover. With the decisional flexibility, organizations can quickly reverse or change the decision, adjusting with the situation. This is an era of lean management, which requires organizations to operate in an environment of flexibility. A quick decision-making ability of managers support all such requirements.

- *Skill to attract and retain the talent:* Attraction and retention of talent may not be always possible only with strategic and innovative reward or compensation design. In a knowledge economy, people prefer to stick around the job, which gives them opportunity to learn and grow, helps to align their self-goals with the organizational goals, provides them the right platform to incubate and nurture their creativity, and enables them to translate their creative ideas into action through innovative product or process design. Thus, retention and attraction of talents would be best possible through nurturing of a compelling workplace culture, which among others, provides opportunities to learn, grow, and innovate. To build such environment in the workplace, managers need to acquire the right skill, so that they can help in attraction and retention of talents as a coach and mentor to employees.

- *Skills to predict the future:* As the rate of change in the new millennium is very fast, managers must also acquire skills to predict the future. Through different sources, managers develop their insights to successfully predict the future in different time horizon. They can validate such insights through networking, sharing diverse assumptions with each other, etc. To effectively predict the future, many managers identify certain trigger points in advance and relate the same with different scenarios to predict the future.

- *Skills to integrate technology with the business:* Managers in the new millennium must also gain skill and familiarity with the new technology, to understand how such technology integrates with the business process. For example, without understanding how ERP modules facilitate in decision making, managers would not be able to succeed in the new millennium.

- *Skill to balance the stakeholders' need:* For any organization, stakeholders are diverse, and their interests often conflict. Effective managers must have the requisite skill to balance such multiple and diverse stakeholders' needs through stakeholder analysis.

Final Take

Skill is goal-oriented learned or acquired actions to perform a task. For every job in the organization, some specific skill sets are essential.

(Box continued)

(Box continued)

> With technological changes skill requirements alter, and so do the requirements of the talent profile.
> In the era of technological change and globalization, through skill change or upgrade, organization can also achieve effectiveness and excellence by acquiring talents.
> For talent acquisition and talent acquisition planning, organizations need to design skill inventories with detailing of the information on the employees.
> Multi-skilling is training employees on different skill sets, so that they can be used for multitasking.
> People with multiple skill sets become more talented, and this is why we say multi-skilling change the talent-mix, and enhance the competitive strength of the organization.
> Partnership and collaborations skills, quick decision-making skills, skills to attract and retain the talent, skills to predict the future, skills to integrate technology with the business, and skills to balance the stakeholders' need are some of the new generation skill sets, which we expect in newly acquired talents.

Developing Competencies for In-house Talent

Competencies are a set of behaviors, which encompass skills, knowledge, abilities, and attributes. Competencies need to be assessed at organization level and at individual level. Individual competencies together reinforce organizational competencies. Individual competencies together reinforce organizational competencies. Incongruence between individual and organizational set of competencies often affects the talent profile. Also this situation indicates organizations have failed to integrate or align the business and strategies with the competency requirements, creating imbalance in the organizational talent pipeline. Depending on the business requirements, and strategic focus, organizations design their competency model from time to time. Such competency model spells out functional requirements for individual employees. Employees in the process can then self-initiate their development, which in the process contributes to talent development of the organization. Through development of competencies, therefore, it is possible for the organization to meet their present and future talent requirements, and simultaneously achieve success.

Developing leadership competencies is considered as one of the important talent development initiatives of the organizations. Most of the organizations have their "future leadership programs" for incubating future leadership talents. In addition due to increased spate of globalization, organizations are now also developing cross-cultural competencies. Here we are detailing on these two competencies, which can benefit organizations making available talents for the future.

Leadership Competencies

Competencies are a desired set of skills, knowledge, attitudes, underlying characteristics, or behavior that differentiates effective performers from ineffective ones (Boyatzis, 1982; McLagan, 1996). Competency-based leadership approach requires organizations to identify the appropriate leadership skills and behaviors that enhance the performance of the organizations. Also, once the competencies are identified, organizations can also use it for developing future leaders. While there are some generic leadership competencies, common for every leader in every organization, organizations also need to identify their specific leadership attributes, which can enhance their competitive advantages. Such identified leadership attributes are then used for identifying the set of competencies required for their leaders.

McCall and Hollenbeck (2002) identified some universal set of leadership competencies as given:

- open-mindedness and flexibility in thoughts and tactics;
- cultural interest and sensitivity;
- ability to deal with complexity
- resilience, resourcefulness, optimism, and energy;
- honesty and integrity;

- stable personal life; and
- value-added technical or business skills.

Cross-cultural Leadership

Globalization has increased the cross-border trades and exchanges, increasing cross-cultural interactions in organizations across the globe. Many international researchers today acknowledge the importance of cross-cultural leadership. Some of the researchers even came out with global-leadership competency model to guide the organizations to equip their leaders on cross-cultural interactions. Although we do not have any agreed definitions on leadership, but we have more or less consensus that leadership is a process of exerting influence on the behavior of others. Influence of culture on leadership has to be understood in terms of contributions of Hofstede (1980), who had seen culture as the collective program of the mind, which differentiates one group of people from another. Cross-cultural leadership, therefore, exerts influence on the behavior of culturally different group of people to achieve some goals. Example of a cross-cultural leader, therefore, is an expatriate leader. Many organizations require their managers and leaders to manage their activities across several countries. Hence, developing cross-cultural leadership competence is now considered important, else they may fail in delivering the results. The scope of cross-cultural leadership even varies within a country, because of the differences in regional culture and diversity.

Cross-cultural leadership styles follow either emic or etic approaches (Akiga & Lowee, 2004). Emic approach considers one culture at a particular point of time to map the leadership behaviors. For example, understanding the culture of Kazakhstan by an Indian manager or leader for effective management of people there to achieve results is an emic approach. Etic approach, on the contrary, takes into account multiple cultures at one point of time to map the leadership behaviors. For example, an Indian leader managing international operations, spread across several countries, has to develop cross-cultural leadership competence, following an etic approach.

Final Take

Incongruence between individual and organizational set of competencies affects the talent profile. Also, this situation indicates organizations have failed to integrate or align the business and strategies creating imbalance in the organizational talent pipeline.

Through development of competencies it is possible for the organization to meet their present and future talent requirements, and simultaneously achieve success.

Developing leadership competencies is considered as one of the important talent development initiatives of the organizations.

Due to increased spate of globalization, organizations are now also developing cross-cultural competencies.

Multiple Talent Assessment Tools

To ensure a foolproof talent acquisition process, organizations, across the globe make use of multiple talent assessment tools, in addition to some of the techniques already explained. Here we explain some of these widely used tools.

Assessment Center Method

Assessment center approach helps in talent identification within the organization. It evaluates the behavior of people using several exercises and games, observations and interviews primarily simulating the real-life situations. It also uses multiple observers for evaluation. Several evaluations are pooled in a meeting where the assessors reach a consensus on the evaluation report of each participant on the assessment process. Assessment center reports can be subjected to statistical tests and validation and can also be used for the purpose of recruitment and selection. In each assessment center, number of participants may vary from five to twenty. More than 20 participants in one assessment center may create problem. The term assessment center is used to indicate extended assessments in a single center or a venue.

Under this method multiple assessors assess talent profiles of people using multiple criteria. Number of assessors and nature of criteria vary widely with the level of the people for whom the talent is assessed. Role play, business simulation and game, leaderless discussions, etc., are more appropriate for senior level people, while interview and paper pencil tests are more suitable for entry level executives. With focus on assessing performances of employees both individually and collectively, this method of performance evaluation and talent assessment facilitates in measuring multiple skill sets, such as:

- interpersonal skills,
- planning and organizing ability,
- innovation,
- stress management, and
- decision-making capability.

Obviously the process helps in proper talent identification inside the organization. Many organizations also make use of assessment center method for developing talents in the organization.

Uses of assessment centers

- Recruitment and selection
- Promotion and other rewards
- Identification of leaders
- Identification of self-directed team members and followers
- Potential appraisal
- Identification of Training and development
- Matching competent people for jobs
- Organizational development
- Skill/competency development

Human Asset Accounting Method

This method attaches money value to people employed with the organization. The process estimates the goodwill value of people or human resources, based on measurement of some variables. Such variables can be either key variables or intervening variables. Key variables are organizational policies and decision-making styles, strategies, skills of people, etc. Intervening variables are those which strengthen the key variables to achieve the desired level of performance. These are loyalties, attitudes, motivations, interpersonal relations, communication, etc. Measuring such variables can quantify human assets, which are otherwise difficult. This helps us to approximate the value of talent in the organization. Tracking the movement of the talent value of the organization, it can take appropriate decisions.

Commonly Used Tools for Talent Acquisition

Organizations make use of a number of tools for talent acquisition. These tools are effectively used both for the new hires and sourcing talents within the organization. Such tools are primarily used for assessing the behavioral or attitudinal compatibility of the targeted talents, so that they can perfectly match with the job and the organization. Some of these commonly used tools are discussed in the following sections.

Behaviorally Anchored Rating Scales (BARS)

Using this assessment method, we can also track the underlying performance behavior for correct assessment of the performance outcome. The process requires developing some attitude and value laden statements. Using a five-point scale (usually it is five-point) answers to such statements are measured to assess the performance behavior. It is important to understand BARS are not to track the performance results as such, rather more specific to track the underlying performance behavior, attitude, and values. From these perspectives, BARS are also effective in potential measurement. Since this system is time-consuming and painstaking, despite its advantages, organizations try to avoid this.

BARS are developed with some effective or ineffective behavioral statements. We call it behaviorally anchored as it represents a continuum of descriptive behavioral statements whose value ranges from least to the most effective. While designing BARS, following steps are followed:

- Document the important performance dimensions of job or jobs.
- Identify some critical incidents that explain effective and ineffective behavior.
- Relate identified effective and ineffective behavior to the required performance dimensions.
- Assign numerical values to each such performance dimension.

Behavioral Observation Scales (BOS)

BOS is frequency rating of critical incidents pertaining to workers' performance. Latham and Kenneth (1977) developed BOS, as they perceived that both the graphic rating scales and BARS require supervisors to make vague judgments. Here, managers rank the list of critical performance-related desired or undesired work issues or incidents based on its occurrence number of times. Using a five-point scale, such frequency of behavior can be measured. For example, a scale like this may be of use: never; rare; sometimes; often; or very often.

Some examples of BOS may be as under:

Time spent for developing subordinates' talent affect my work.
_____

When subordinates underperform, I try to assess their development needs. _____

My subordinates always look for their self-development opportunities. _____

Talent attrition in my organization is attributable to our work environment. _____

Mixed Standard Scales (MSS)

MSS helps us to measure good, average, and poor performance referring to specific job-related behaviors. Its uses differ depending on the performance dimension. For example, for a marketing person, customer relations, knowledge about market intelligence, etc., could be the important performance dimensions. But in case of a finance manager, such performance dimension varies. MSS primarily focuses on mapping the concrete observable job-related behavior, based on which simple judgment on performance management related issues can be made. The unique feature of MSS is that it measures performance-based examples of behavior from three dimensions, that is, good, average, and poor. Thus, each performance dimension has three statements (good, average, and poor), MSS need to have nine statements, three for each of the statement; to measure effective or ineffective job-related performance behaviors. To get better results, MSS is randomly mixed, as it substantially reduces the rater errors.

This method, therefore, evaluates traits with three specific descriptions of each trait. These descriptions indicate performance levels, conforming to each trait. Questions are randomly arranged to prevent any rating bias. Therefore in character, this scale is essentially a trait approach to performance appraisal, where measurement is done on the basis of comparison in three dimensions, indicating better than, equal to, or worse than to measure the level of performance.

Example of a mixed standard scale is given below:

Mixed standard scale

DIRECTIONS: Please indicate whether the individual's performance is better than (+), equal to (0), or worse (–) than each of the following standards.

1. ____ Generally agrees and cooperates with others (equal to: in COOPERATION).

(Box continued)

(Box continued)

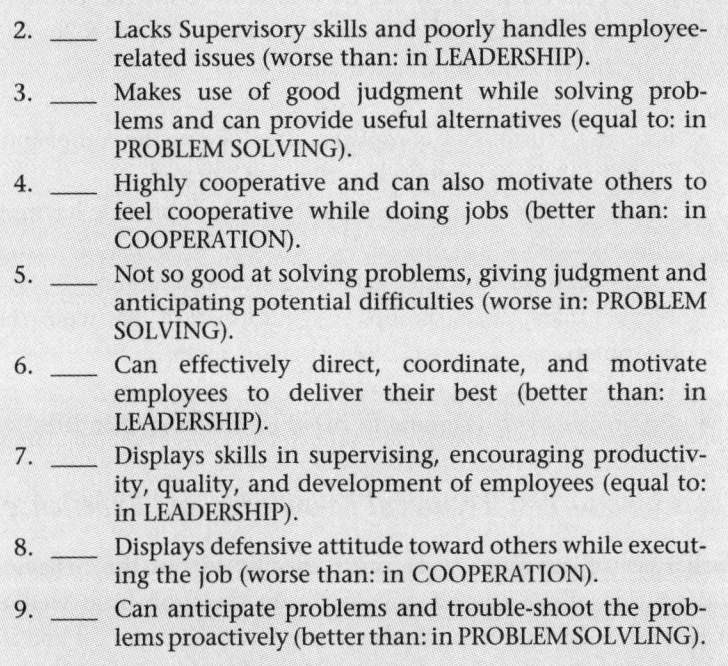

2. _____ Lacks Supervisory skills and poorly handles employee-related issues (worse than: in LEADERSHIP).

3. _____ Makes use of good judgment while solving problems and can provide useful alternatives (equal to: in PROBLEM SOLVING).

4. _____ Highly cooperative and can also motivate others to feel cooperative while doing jobs (better than: in COOPERATION).

5. _____ Not so good at solving problems, giving judgment and anticipating potential difficulties (worse in: PROBLEM SOLVING).

6. _____ Can effectively direct, coordinate, and motivate employees to deliver their best (better than: in LEADERSHIP).

7. _____ Displays skills in supervising, encouraging productivity, quality, and development of employees (equal to: in LEADERSHIP).

8. _____ Displays defensive attitude toward others while executing the job (worse than: in COOPERATION).

9. _____ Can anticipate problems and trouble-shoot the problems proactively (better than: in PROBLEM SOLVLING).

Based on the interpretation of the responses, we can assess the talents and the potentiality of the people, and accordingly plan for their future development.

Behavioral Checklist Method

Under this method the rater checks the standard behavioral statements, indicates some performance dimensions or the other. This method is perhaps the oldest technique of performance appraisal, but since the rating is two-dimensional, somewhat like yes/no, its reliability and validity is often questioned. It is more applicable to map the employees' developmental needs. The results are better when it is used to describe the behavior of the subordinates, rather than rating. Its major operational difficulty is to develop the proper instruments and relate the same to the employees' performance criteria. A behavioral statement may indicate both the effective and ineffective job-related behaviors. Let us examine the following randomly chosen behavioral statements:

- Attends to customers' complaints after logging the complaints.
- Talks to the employees when they are agitated.
- Always prefers those job assignments which provide learning opportunities.
- Takes decision only after gathering facts and figures.
- Never manipulates company's information to woo the customers.
- Plans before starting of a job.
- Prioritizes work assignments based on the boss' mandates.

Questions to Test Technical Knowledge and Experience

Earlier set of questions were more specific to test the behavior and attitude of the targeted talents to test their job-fit as well as organization-fit. But each job also requires certain technical knowledge and experience. To test such technical knowledge and experience, we may also design some standard questionnaires as under.

- Indicate the type of activities you have participated during last six months, which you deem to have increased your technical knowledge.
- How can such technical knowledge be integrated with the existing job?
- Keeping in view your current job, indicate some of the likely future changes, and how you prepare yourself for the same.
- From your past experience with a job, list out some of the important job-related issues, which you feel are problems. Also mention how did you overcome such job-related problems?
- Did you participate in any project during last year? What was your role? What problems and issues did you face in the job?

- To reduce some job-related problems, what types of skills and expertise did you use during last year?
- Can you think of some technologies that can improve your job?
- Mention some of your important learning from the job mistakes.
- List some of your important achievements that make you feel proud.

Questions for Testing Leadership/Management Skills

Leadership/Management skills are also important skill sets for employees, particularly for the talented employees. In talent acquisition availability of such skill sets in new hires, and internal hiring can be tested using some standard questions as under.

- Explain your management philosophy.
- Explain how you translate your management philosophy into practices.
- Describe an incident when you had to put your espoused management philosophy to test.
- After this incident was it necessary for you to revisit your espoused management philosophy and bring changes?
- In your work situation you have management teams. Explain a situation that describes your team spirit.
- In your workplace you have come across many work-related conflicts. Describe a situation when you had to resolve conflicts emanated from your managing a team.
- How do you motivate and sustain productive environment while managing change in your work situation?
- In managing change in your work situation, describe important challenges that you have faced.
- How did you manage technological change in your work situation? Describe the process adopted by you.
- In your work situation, you have to manage difficult employees. Describe a situation explaining your management of difficult employees.

Analytical Skills

In acquiring talents, we also focus on analytical skills. Hence, testing the analytical skills of new talents before hiring, helps us to meet the talent gap in the organization. Some standard questions for testing analytical skills are presented below.

- Describe your experience in handling complaints, including handling of grievances of your team members.
- Describe a situation when your recommended course of action was not accepted by a customer. Explain what you did then.
- Describe a situation when your recommended course of action was not accepted by your team member. Explain what you did then.
- In doing your job, what type of problem solving and decision making is required? Explain this with both subjective and objective inputs.
- Recollect a situation when your decisions were reversed. Narrate the consequences and your action after that.
- Describe a case of failure at your work situation. How did it affect you thereafter?
- Describe a case of your action that led to improvement of process in your organization? Narrate your specific contribution in this case.

Likewise depending on your specific organization needs you can develop your questions to test the technical, functional, and general knowledge and skills of the targeted talents, who may be new hires or hired from in-house. These questions are just one possible way of assessing potential talents so that risk of wrong hiring is minimized, but it cannot guarantee that newly hired talents based on the responses of this questionnaire will give you the improved performance and productivity. Many world-class organizations today focus more on behavior and attitude compatibility. Such organizations have their structured programs for talent incubation.

Final Take

Organizations make use of multiple talent assessment tools to ensure a foolproof talent acquisition process.

Assessment center approach helps in identification of talents within the organizations. Under this method multiple assessors assess talent profile of people using multiple criteria.

Human asset accounting method attaches money value to people employed with the organization, which approximates the value of talent in the organization.

BARS, using some attitude and value-laden statements, measure potential talents.

BOS also helps in measuring the talents by measuring the critical incidents pertaining to workers' performance.

MSS helps us to measure good, average, and poor performance referring to specific job-related behaviors, based on which we can measure the talent profile.

Behavioral checklist method based on checking the standard behavioral statements indicates some performance dimensions, which also help us in assessing the talent profile.

Organizations can also design some structured questionnaire to test technical knowledge and experience, leadership, managerial skills, and analytic skills of potential talents.

Talent acquisition in Indian companies: Lessons from Wipro

To drive the growth metrics, Wipro continues to focus on talent acquisition. Wipro Ltd is a leader in IT and Business Process consulting, and an ardent believer of "business through technology." The company believes such approach helps their clients to be more adaptive and successful in business. Globally recognized for innovation in business solutions, with current headcount of 156,866 employees, and revenues of US$7.3 billion (2014), the company now operates from 175 locations of the world, encompassing almost the entire globe.

To sustain in competition at the global space, the company now commits for global talent acquisition, creating a special role

(Box continued)

(Box continued)

of the Global Head for talent acquisition. This special job role requires sourcing talents for all verticals and geographies. The company believes leadership talent requires not just commitment for work, but also the fire within. Such fire manifests in action, in energy, and in knowledge of the Wiproites.

Driven by such intensity to win and nurture talent, Wipro provides entrepreneurial and performance-driven work environment. This ensures in-house talent sourcing for future leadership roles. Apart from this, global talent sourcing team of the company continuously tracks talented professionals in the industry. The global talent sourcing team not only focuses on talent acquisition with open invitation to those who feel they have fire within, but also extends their support to visit such prospective talents for insular discussion, to ensure that they take an informed choice to join Wipro.

With focus on biodiversity to make Wipro Headquarter a destination for migratory butterflies, the company's economic sustainability has now embedded the culture of diversity. With 30 percent female workforce, and little less than 1 percent physically challenged, the company today reiterates their commitment to talents with diversity neutrality.

A winner of NASSCOM's Corporate Award for Excellence in Diversity and Inclusion in 2014, Wipro continues its commitment to customers' success and innovation. All these could help the company to make their talent acquisition pursuit an ongoing and globally recognized initiative.

Summing up

Talent acquisition is an ongoing process that aims to attract, find, and select highly talented individuals.

Talent acquisition is now managed strategically integrating learning and development and workforce planning functions of the organizations.

Scope of talent acquisition now even extends to acquiring companies. Such acquisitions are not for extension of business value chain; rather it is for getting the talented people.

Talent analytics, dashboard, social networking sites, head-hunting, brand building, organization-fit and job-fit analysis, etc., are some of the effective talent acquisition tools used by the organizations.

Many organizations also use competency-based approach in acquiring talent.

Some organizations also acquire new startups, particularly those which are failed to acquire their talents on long-term basis.

Talent acquisition from in-house potential candidates is also gradually gaining importance.

Tyco's New Recruitment Paves the Process of Talent Acquisition

Tyco, the US$10 billion Safety and Security Company with 65,000 headcounts spread across 1,000 locations of the world, due to their typical nature of business does not always get new talents from the market for lateral engagement. The company emphasizes more on developing talent within. To ensure that in-house talent pipeline is effective, the company emphasizes the entry level recruitments are made with a long-term perspectives. From such new recruits potential talents are identified and developed through effective talent development initiatives. The entry level recruitment, in addition to rigorous interview, also tests the job role and culture-fit of the candidates, so that such recruits can quickly relate with the organization, gain the sense of pride, and become more productive.

To strengthen the long-term relationships with the new recruits, the on-boarding process emphasizes more and more on cultural alignment of the new recruits, so that they get tuned with the value systems of the organization, and come out successfully with the desired performance behavior. The company also believes in diversity-inclusion practices, and integrates this with the organizational practices in general, and business practices in particular.

(Case Study continued)

(Case Study continued)

Employee engagement is achieved by aligning the activities of the new recruits with the strategy of the organization, and helping them to trace how their contributions fit in achieving the organizational goals. Gradually such employees feel more loyal and committed to the organization. Tyco believes that employee engagement is a continuous process, hence it should start with the process of onboarding and continue till the employees work with the organization, that is, covering the entire employment life cycle of the employees with Tyco.

Similarly, the company also emphasizes on competency-based goal setting for the employees, so each employee can feel that they are contributing to the value chain of the organization. This promotes the feeling of self-worth, and makes them more confident and matured.

Hence, the talent development process in Tyco is not just limited to few identified potential employees, but to all who are recruited at the base level, and then gradually developed for organizational talent pipeline. This is a unique example of in-house talent acquisition focusing on in-house talent development.

This case study has been developed based on the website inputs of the company.

Bibliography

Akiga, B., & Lowe, K. (2004). Cross-cultural leadership. In G. Goethals, G. Sorenson, & J. Burns (Eds), *Encyclopedia of leadership*. Thousand Oaks, CA: SAGE, pp. 301–307.

Ambrose, M. L., Anaud, A., & Schminke, M. (2011). Individual moral development and ethical climate: The influence of person–organization fit on job attitudes. *Journal of Business Ethics*, 77, 323–333.

Bhatnagar, J. (2007). Talent management strategy of employee engagement of Indian ITES employees: Key to retention. *Employee Relations*, 29(6), 640–663.

Bhattacharyya, D. K. (2011). *Performance management systems and strategies*. Pearson: New Delhi.

Boyatzis, R. E. (1982). *The competent manager: A model for effective performance*. New York: John Wiley.

Cappelli, P. (2008). Talent Management for the Twenty-First Century. *Harvard Business Review, 86*(3), 74-81.

Cheese, P. (2010). Talent management for a new era: What we have learned from the recession and what we need to focus on next. *Human Resource Management International Digest, 18*(3), 3-5.

Davenport, T. H., Harris, J., & Shapiro, J. (2010). Competing on talent analytics. *Harvard Business Review, 88*(10), 52-58.

Fitz-enz, J. (2000). *The ROI human capital: Measuring the economic value of employee performance*. New York, NY: American Management Association.

Heger, B. K. (2007). Linking the employment value proposition (EVP) to employee engagement and business outcomes: Preliminary findings from a linkage research pilot study. *Organization Development Journal, 25*(2), 21–33.

Hofstede, G. (1980). *Culture's consequences: International differences in work related values*. London: SAGE.

Latham, Gary P., & Kenneth, N. Wexley. (1977). Behavioural observation scales for performance appraisal purposes. *Personnel Psychology, 30*(2), 255–268.

McCall, M., & Hollenbeck, G. (2002). *Developing global executives: The lessons of international experience*. Boston, MA: Harvard Business School Publishing.

Malcolm, C., McCulloch, Daniel B., & Turban (2007). Using person-organization fit to select employees for high-turnover jobs. *International Journal of Selection and Assessment, 15*(1), 63–71.

McLagan, P. (1996). Great ideas revisited. *Training & Development, 50*(1), 60–66.

3

Nurturing Talent

Introduction

In India developing the talent pipeline for ensuring continuity of talent supply within the organization is always an integral business practice for Tata, HUL, ITC, and public sector enterprises like SAIL, ONGC, etc. Other organizations followed the practice of lateral hire for meeting their time to time talent requirements. However, with increased spate of competition, particularly after global mobility of talents, many organizations have now changed their traditional practices, and focus on incubating talent in-house for building their talent pipeline. Taking the new hires through robust onboarding, including cross-functional induction is now almost common for large companies in India. For example, Vodafone has 45-day cross-functional induction program for the newcomers. Tata has their flagship leadership development programs, known as Tata Administrative Services (TAS). Similarly HUL has their world class leadership development program. In both these organizations talent development process has been institutionalized. Hence, Indian companies are now reviewing their talent development strategies to avoid the future leadership crisis.

Building talent pipeline by rehiring former executives has again become an institutionalized practice for Indian companies. Infosys, Tata, HUL, ITC are known for such practices. For Infosys this is "Green Channel Hiring." With such new initiatives, and renewed focus on developing in-house talent, future talent pipeline for Indian companies is expected to look bright.

Browsing literatures on talent and talent management, we observe general consensus in corporate circles is that talent can provide competitive advantage to organizations. Also, we find the acknowledgment of the fact that talent is scarce, and organizations across the world have to compete for it. Although conventionally we define talent as mental power, a natural endowment, an aptitude, ability, a natural capacity or a special gift, that is, talent is inborn; recent studies indicated that with inborn talent we cannot achieve results in organizations. An organization requires development and utilization of talent to achieve results. Thus, organizations even though may acquire talent through new recruitment, cannot achieve results, unless such talents are continuously developed, pacing with the changing business needs and strategies. Also organizations may not always achieve success in acquiring or hiring new talents through recruitment. It may not be a cost-effective solution also. Talent development in such cases can incubate in-house talent. The scope of talent development therefore extends to incubation of in-house talents, and developing the newly hired talents, pacing with the changing needs and strategies of the organizations.

In organizations talents may not restrict to senior leadership. Its scope extends to all cross-sections of employees. Holistic talent development, therefore, requires developing a talent driven organization culture. Ultimate goal of talent development is to ensure that people with requisite skills and aptitudes are available with the organizations, both for meeting present and future requirements. Some of the activities that encompass talent development include:

- Review of talent in terms of organizational existing talent management process. Talent management process encompasses all activities related to talent attraction, acquisition, retention, and development. Hence, it covers succession planning, designing of talent development programs, alignment of talent needs with the business goals, and strategies of the organization, etc.
- Helping organizations to develop talents; pacing with business goals and strategies.
- Developing talent enrichment plans to build leadership quality among the potential employees to future leadership roles.

- Performing all the supporting activities of talent development, like performance and potential evaluation, job rotations, assessments, training, coaching, mentoring, etc.
- Creating talent pipeline for meeting present and future talent requirements of the organization.
- Calibrating talent development plans with the changing business plans and strategies of the organizations.

Final Take

Talent is scarce, and organizations across the world have to compete for it.

Organizations have to continuously develop talent pacing with the changing business needs and strategies.

The scope of talent development extends to incubation of in-house talents, and developing the newly hired talents, pacing with the changing needs and strategies of the organizations.

Holistic talent development requires developing a talent-driven organization culture.

Talent pipeline in organizations has to meet both the present and future talent requirements of the organization.

Talent development plans need to be calibrated from time to time as per the changing business plans and strategies of the organizations.

Requirements for Talent Development

Haskins and Shaffer (2010) suggested that talent development process should be business driven, future focused, integrated, and capable to deliver measurable results. Based on their studies, Haskins and Shaffer suggested four components of talent development process. These are:

- understanding what drives business of the organization;
- ensuring employees' develop those identified talents that drive business;

- making talent development as an ongoing and continuous learning process; and
- measuring the results of talent development.

Following this process, organizations can develop talent. However, on drawing lessons from the organizations, we observe that while considering their talent development programs, organizations broadly consider following issues:

- nature of markets;
- global perspectives;
- competitive advantage;
- economic value creation and metrics;
- culture; and
- leadership.

Considering these issues, organizations can draw plans for talent development, duly identifying specific skills, attributes, and knowledge requirements of the employees. Such identified knowledge requirements on one hand help in achieving the business goals of the organizations, and at the same time help in detailing learning and development programs for talent development.

We reiterate that skills, attributes, and knowledge requirements are specific to the organizations and their business plans. Such requirements may also vary within an organization with the shift in their business focus. Hence, once talent for the employees is developed by the organizations, it does not mean it will suffice the purpose of the organizations for ever. Employees' talents need to be revisited and calibrated from time to time, and accordingly talent development activities need to be continued.

Detailed learning and development plan for the employees to develop their talent can be both instruction-based and experience-based. Instruction-based methods include in-house training, or training through hiring of external training providers, and self-paced programmed instructions, like e-training or computer-based training (CBT). Experience-based methods, on the other hand, include coaching, mentoring, and new job assignments. Although we do not have any empirical evidence on the effectiveness of learning and development methods for talent development, it is said that experience-based approach to talent development works better. However, we cannot discredit the instruction-based approach to learning and development for talent development, particularly when employees are to be taken through new areas of skills, knowledge, and attributes, pacing with the changing needs of the market and business environment in general. Hence, better approach to talent development would be more balanced rather than only instruction-based or experience-based. Thus, for talent development, one learning and development method complements the other. Both are critical and equally important for holistic talent development in the organizations. Based on these discussions, therefore, we can say, talent development is a multidimensional activity in organization, and it requires careful planning.

Scullion and Collings (2011) defined TM as an integrated and strategic process of organizations to attract, select, develop, and manage employees. Talent development, on the other hand, represents an important component of the overall talent management process (Cappelli, 2008; Novations, 2009). While it is possible for organizations to pursue a strategy that focuses on talent acquisition from the external labor market, such a strategy is unlikely to be successful in the long term. It is well established that organizations can gain significant advantages from internal talent development approach. But to make internal talent development program successful, organizations need to acquire and develop industry and firm-specific knowledge and skills (Lepak & Snell, 1999). This requires organizations to make significant investments in talent development activities, so that internal talent development capabilities of the organizations can be built and organizations can make its effective use. Talent development activities in the organization have to be undertaken in such a way so that they can ensure that there is zero talent attrition, more planned succession, and simultaneous brand building of the organization (Gandz, 2006).

To understand the scope of talent development, we try to answer the following questions:

- What talent organization wishes to develop?
- By developing such talent, how can organization meet its business goals and strategies?
- Does organizational talent development process focus on technical or generic competencies, or both?
- Does organizational talent development process focus on individual-level talent development or organization level talent development, or combines both?
- Does organization follow accelerated talent development or talent development in a normal way?

Answering the above questions, organizations can successfully draw their talent development programs, in alignment with their business goals and strategies. Also such talent development programs are more integrated and can truly benefit in developing talent pipeline to ensure present and future flow of talent in the organization.

Final Take

Talent development process should be business driven, future focused, integrated, and capable of delivering measurable results.

While developing talent development programs, organizations broadly consider issues like nature of markets, global perspectives, competitive advantages, economic value creation, culture, and leadership.

Organizations also consider how identified talent issues help in achieving the business goals of the organizations and at the same time help in detailing learning and development programs for talent development.

Talent development plan can be both instruction-based and experience-based.

Talent development is a multi-dimensional activity in the organization, and it requires careful planning.

Defining Talent for Development Purposes

We have already stated that organizational definition of talent widely varies. Imagine the case of your organization. You may observe your organization emphasizes more on compliance with ethics, social responsiveness, customer services, etc., as important talent attributes. Contrarily, you may observe another organization that perceives talent as fast-pacing performance track record, target achievement, etc. These two definitional differences on talent obviously focus on talent development functions differently. However, we have a general consensus that talent is exemplary qualities that a person possesses. Let us understand it citing some references from our literature survey. Gladwell (2010) defined talent is our aggregated knowledge and skills that we acquire over our 10 years' or 10,000 hours specific job experience. Michaels, Handfield-Jones, and Axelrod (2001) conceptualized talent as those attributes of leaders and managers which can drive the performance, and at the same time help the organization to achieve the business goals. Such talent attributes as observed by them are sharp strategic mind, leadership ability, emotional maturity, communications skills, the ability to attract and inspire other talented people, entrepreneurial instincts, fundamental skills, and the ability to deliver results. Ready, Conger, and Hill (2010), on the other hand, defined talent as those attributes which can ensure credible and consistent performance delivery.

With these arguments, we can say that organizations focus on talent development strategically, either with inclusive or exclusive approach, both for improved performance results and Return on Investment (ROI).

Final Take

Definition of talents varies across organizations. Based on such variation in definitions of talent, organizations focus on talent development functions differently.

(Box continued)

(Box continued)

We have some general consensus on the definition of talents, that is, exemplary qualities, and attribute that drive performance and help organizations to achieve business goals.

Effective HR Systems to Support Development of Talent

HR planning, recruitment, performance management, career management, learning and development, and succession planning are important HR systems which support development of talent in the organizations. Scholars like Dickmann, Brewster, and Sparrow (2011), McDonnell and Collings (2011), Avedon and Scholes (2010), and Kaye (2002) have recommended various components of HR systems, which can support development of talent. For example, McDonnell and Collings (2011) recommended adopting a contingency approach while factoring HR systems for talent development. Contingency approach obviously accounts for strategy issues, stakeholders' interest, etc., while drawing talent development plans.

Talent development programs in organizations may be formal, relationship based, job based or informal. Wilson et al. (2011) recommended such a talent development program with 70 percent emphasis on the job, 20 percent emphasis on relationships, and rest 10 percent based on formal developmental activities. However, many scholars have criticized this model of talent development, for it has too much emphasis on learning from experience. In fact suggestions are to emphasize more on learning through formal development programs, which may be conceptual and skills-based training, personal growth laboratories, etc. (Conger, 2010). Such talent development programs emphasize more on developing generic skills. Coaching, mentoring, counseling, etc., are relationship-based talent development programs.

What would be more appropriate for the organization depends more on the specific needs, priorities, and strategies. Thus, we do not have any stringent mandate for 70:20:10 model of talent development.

Your Take—For C-suite

Toyota believes every activity in the organization is their new learning opportunities. The company believes every manager is a teacher, and developing people is their top-most priority. Such ingrained culture of Toyota could make the best in developing exceptional talent and retaining them. Toyota believes their exceptional people are their only competitive strength. They don't believe that talent is innate, rather they believe even a poor performer can be transformed to a talent for the company. May be 10 percent is innate talent, but 90 percent can be developed, is what the company feels. The underlying philosophy of Toyota' talent development includes long-term business focus, standardized processes, select those for development who understand the work, develop those who follow company's philosophy, respect suppliers challenging them and helping them to improve, and relentlessly focus on continuous development.

Coaching and Mentoring for Talent Development

Coaching and mentoring reinforce talent development functions in organization. Success of coaching and mentoring greatly depends on how organizations value their employee development programs.

Coaching as a talent development program is more suitable for those who are already identified as potential talent for the organization. Through coaching, such potential employees gain insights on managing their performance autonomously. Organizations which value such talent development program may make use of both internal and external coaches. Internal coaches are those who have already acquired such proficiency through their own phase of development. For organizations internal coaching is more cost effective; also such internal coaches can better relate their coaching, pacing with organizational talent development priorities.

External coaches on the other hand are professional coaches, who are hired for coaching the employees. Use of external coaches is recommended only in the areas of coaching for which organizations have the constraint of internal coaches.

Mentoring also complements the talent development process like coaching. Mentoring is more effective than coaching, as it is more specific to identified individual, who is constantly guided on one to one basis in understanding the criticalities of the jobs, and then gradually reach to the level of expected performance. Organizations only invest in mentoring for those identified talents who will continue with them on long-term basis, as it involves more cost than coaching. Mentoring can be both non-directive and sponsored. For a mentee, non-directive mentor is a role model. He/she follows the mentor to replicate the knowledge and skill, and in the process develop the required competencies. Contrary to mentoring, using a sponsored model literally makes the mentor responsible for the talent development of mentees (assigned to him/her). Organizational practices, however, suggest, it is always better to have a mix approach in talent development.

Final Take

Coaching and mentoring reinforce talent development functions in organization.

Coaching as a talent development program is more suitable for those who are already identified as potential talent for the organization.

Mentoring is more effective than coaching, as it is more specific to identified individual, who is constantly guided on one to one basis in understanding the criticalities of the jobs, and then gradually reach to the level of expected performance.

Value Chain Analysis of Talent Development

Value chain refers to adding value to the chain of activities within a firm's operations. Usually value chain analysis is done at the departmental level or even at the activity level. The underlying idea is that when products and services pass through different chain of activities, it can gain value at each activity level when we manage such activity in efficient and cost-effective manner. Extending Michael Porter's arguments on value chain (1985) to talent development process of an organization, we can understand how talent acquisition, retention, and management can be important support activities in talent development value chain and how it can generate value. In talent development process value chain analysis helps in identifying our business activity within the process that contributes to organizational overall competitive strategy. Also it helps us to assess efficiencies and cost savings to be gained within the process. Organization may gain cost competitiveness through value chain analysis by reducing the cost of the individual activities within the value chain or by reconfiguring the value chain.

For value chain analysis of talent development process of any organization, following steps are important:

- *Identify or clarify our overall competitive strategy:* This may mean revisiting our vision and mission, or reiterating our short-term and long-term goals, ensuring that everyone within all departments in the organization is on the same line of thought.
- *Activity analysis:* Identify each activity undertaken in the talent-management process (acquiring, retaining, and developing of human capital). This can be done by conducting a brainstorming session or a business process review with key individuals. Key individuals are responsible for carrying out the activities and they are also impacted by these activities.
- *Value analysis:* Assess value of each activity that it brings to the process. Understand the implications of the process changes, not only from the specific departmental perspectives, but also from the perspectives of all other departments of the organization. Finally, evaluate the overall impact of proposed changes.
- *Planning:* Develop strategic plan to reduce the costs of the activities within the talent development value chain, explore the value adding potentialities, and reconfigure.

We can also apply these steps to the recruitment component of the talent management value chain ensuring that the recruitment process supports the activity of attracting right-fit employees, that is, those who can support the organization to achieve its strategic intents. Let us assume we look for customer-service skills in such new talents. Likewise we perform the activity analysis, involving cross-functional expertise of people, and try to understand where we can optimize the cost, and where we can add value to the activities. Make a primary evaluation of our amended value chain, in terms of its efficacy, cost savings, value addition, etc., even stretching beyond our departmental boundaries.

Make the secondary evaluation in terms of relational value chain. For example, in-house talent development plans for operators, utilizing the operation people, in one way may reduce the cost and generate better value, but at the same time may reduce the productivity and performance of these in-house trainers, as they need to remain absent from their regular operation jobs. It means cost savings in one department add to the monetary costs to another department. Finally, develop the strategic plan to reduce the costs and reconfigure the value chain.

Such strategic plan is expected to ensure that suggested changes in the activities of the value chain will have incremental effect on the competitive strategies of the organization. Also, such strategic plan must reflect the inputs from all affected players from within and outside the department. It will also have a realistic timeline for implementation and results, provision for utilization of talents, provisions for measurement of results, and finally it will also focus on continuous talent development activities across the value chain.

With an effective value chain analysis for talent development, we can assess how activities centering on talent development contribute to the internal value chain of the organization, and enhance its competitive strength. Competitive strength from talent development value chain is obtained by the organization through the benefit of synergy. Benefits are not just limited to cost savings and efficiency in each activity of the talent development, it can also help in reducing talent attrition, increase in loyalty and commitment to organization, and support the talent engagement programs.

However, some researchers could observe the process of value creation in creative and/or knowledge-intensive organizations, who are engaged in higher rates of innovation (Potts, 2006), are entirely different. Characteristically such organizations believe in more networked structure, facilitating shared innovation, even crossing across the organizational boundary. Some researchers (Hearn, Roodhouse, & Blakey, 2007) believe that in such organizations the term value creating ecology is more important than value chain. Talent development process in creative industries therefore more appropriate when it considers value creating ecology. For value chain, key driver is revenue, and it leverages knowledge within the enterprise for developing talents. On the other hand, knowledge is the key driver for value creating ecology and it leverages knowledge across the ecosystems for talent development.

Final Take

1. Talent acquisition, retention, and management can be important support activities in talent development value chain.
2. In talent development process value chain analysis helps in identifying our business activity within the process that contributes to organizational overall competitive strategy.
3. Organization gains cost competitiveness through value-chain analysis by reducing the cost of the individual activities within the value chain or by reconfiguring the value chain.
4. In creative and/or knowledge-intensive organizations, who believe in more networked structure, facilitating shared innovation, even crossing across the organizational boundary. In such organizations we use the term value creating ecology than value chain.
5. Revenue is the key driver for value chain, and it leverages knowledge within the enterprise for developing talents. On the other hand for value creating ecology, key driver is knowledge, and it leverages knowledge across the ecosystems for talent development.

Talent Development Strategy

Primary talent development strategy is to achieve long-term sustenance and growth of the organizations through enhanced commitment and engagement of talented employees. We have already explained what talent is and how such concept of talent reflects onto various talent development practices of the organization. Integrated talent development, ensuring person–job fit, is another important issue of talent development strategy. Primarily talent development strategies emphasize on long-term focus, integration with the business goals, emphasis on person–job fit, enhancement of employees' commitment and engagement, etc.

To realize above strategic intents, organizations should focus on:

- initiating the talent development process with the process of onboarding;
- systematic training and learning;
- continuous performance reviews;
- systematic person–job fit analysis;
- strengthening employees' engagement programs; and
- simultaneous focus on experiential learning.

Strategic talent development cycle of the organization at the outset starts with the business context of talent development, pacing with the current bench strength of talents in the organization. Then it decides on the appropriate mix of internally and externally available talents in terms of ROI, and then decides the talent development programs, implements the talent development programs, and then review the success.

Companies like Amway, a US$7 billion giant, in relationship marketing strategically focus on employee engagement and performance driven culture along with their talent development strategies to achieve better results.

Final Take

1. Primarily talent development strategies emphasize on long-term focus, integration with the business goals, emphasis on person–job fit, enhancement of employees' commitment and engagement, etc.
2. Strategic talent development cycle of the organization decides on the appropriate mix of internally and externally available talents in terms of ROI, and then decides the talent development programs, implements the talent development programs, and then reviews the success.

ROI of Talent Development Programs

As we have multiple options for talent development, organizations also calculate the ROI while selecting particular talent development program or programs, pacing with its business goals.

ROI from talent development programs follows the analogies of computation which we have explained in Chapter 5. Some of the talent development programs, like coaching and mentoring, are a long drawn process, and results can only be tracked in the long run. But ROI from other talent development methods can be tracked quickly, even immediately after the succeeding performance cycle. Let us take the example of a specific learning and development program, which we have used for development of talent of the organization. Employees who have attended such program, subject to their proper understanding, can put their learned knowledge in practice, tracking which organization can compute the ROI.

Like ROI from talent management (Chapter 5), increased ROI from talent development need not guarantee organizational success. Reasons are attributable to the appropriate fit of the talent development programs for the specific organization. In a steel manufacturing, or a power plant, coaching and mentoring program helps immensely, as in both these cases, specialized knowledge and skills are the important inputs of talent for their employees. Hence, such organizations' investment in talent development (more through coaching and mentoring) programs is much higher than others. Contrarily for a retail organization, for quick transferability of knowledge and skills, investment in talent development is relatively low.

Ethics in Talent Development

Ethical consideration in talent development stems from organizational talent development policies. From ROI perspective, organizations may legitimize exclusive talent development approach, to limit its focus only on those who are identified as future leaders for the organizations. But such practices may be differently interpreted by other employees of the organization. Those who are not covered under talent development programs may feel they are deprived. Gradually their performance and commitment to organization decline. But contrarily when we consider inclusive approach to talent development to cover all cross-sections of employees, we are ethical in one sense, as we are equally committed to the development needs of all. But in the process organizations may lose their cost competitiveness for talent development.

Considering human resources from the asset percepts, we can appreciate the legitimacy of organizational investment on people for talent development, hoping some incremental benefits in terms of performance and productivity. Commitment orientation to human resource management today also requires human resource managers to be the facilitators to develop employees to establish link between individual and organizational goals. In achieving the business results, in organizations, people issues often supersede technologies, strategies, and other operational excellence (Bhattacharyya, 2013). Thus, organizational commitment to talent development is theoretically inseparable from the ROI perspectives, and it is now embedded with the ethical practices. We can therefore say with talent development ethical issues are embedded.

Some ethical issues in talent development are:

- An inclusive approach to talent development, to cover all cross-sections of employees under the talent development programs. This will also help in branding the organization and future talent attraction. Organizations may differentiate talent development activities and investment, in terms of level and identified potentialities of the employees, but cannot altogether truncate it for those who are not identified as potential talents.

- A diversity-neutral talent development approach, so that organizations can free themselves from discriminatory talent development practices, in terms of gender, culture, or any other diversity issues. Many studies have now authenticated the importance of diversity-neutral HRM practices, as we find good talents even in minorities.

- Extend organizational existing ethical guidelines to talent development issues, to ensure its documentation, so that managers engaged in talent development activities can adhere to the ethical issues in doing their jobs.

- Make compliance with the ethical issues as important performance requirements, so that it can reflect also on talent development practices.

- Ensure organizational talent development also contributes to social capital, which can make the organization more socially responsive through the behavior of its leaders, and in the process help in brand building.

Various empirical studies show ethical talent development practices, apart from organizational brand building, can attract new talents and enhance employee engagement. Even the positive word of mouth cascades to customer retention and new market development.

Microsoft aligns diversity and inclusion with their talent development

Microsoft's declared policy is to "reinvent productivity to empower every person and every organization on the planet to

(Box continued)

(Box continued)

do more and achieve more." And for this their strategy is to "maximize the business impact of global diversity and inclusion to empower our people, transform our culture and delight our customers." Microsoft embeds diversity inclusion in all the spheres—people, culture, and customers. The company believes that the workforce diversity helps them to develop pipeline for future leadership positions. Passion for work, desire to make impact in careers, in the community, and on the world are what the company uses for initial phase of talent identification. Since 2001 the company has started recognizing and encouraging technical women, supporting IT education for women, encouraging them to study, etc.

With opportunity to employees to incubate their wild ideas, talent development process gets additional boost. Wide job-mix helps the employees to select their best perceived job, across any country. Individual employees' career and professional development is done in partnership with the managers. With multiple career path options, and facility to move across professions, the company with diversity and inclusion can achieve success in talent development.

Principles for Designing Talent Development Programs

Designing of talent development programs widely varies across the organizations, for their obvious difference in business focus and strategies. Also, it depends on organizational resource capabilities to invest in talent development programs. Similarly time scale for organizational commitment to talent development is also important. For example, some organizations make their investment on talent development only when they go for new technology, while some consider their investment on talent development as an ongoing initiative. Hence, we cannot have any universal principles. However, whatever could be assimilated from the industry practices as principles for designing talent development programs is reproduced below:

- Frame a clear talent policy, which should also clarify the organizational definition on talent. Such documented talent policy will serve as the guideline for design of talent development programs, ensuring consistency, and adherence to organizational philosophies and values to talent.
- Adopt an integrative approach of talent development, suitably defining talent development process. Integrative approach requires all aspects of organizational activities that may align with the talent development process. For example, how new talents can contribute to changed business focus of the organization. Having a compensation and reward policy with more focus on variables linked with scaled performance, may not address the need for customer relationship management (CRM), as the sales people will be busier in delivering sales results. Talent managers, therefore, need to understand all these aspects while designing the talent development programs.
- Focus on talent development both for the present and the future. Change in organizations is continuous. Apart from the major effect of technological change, organizations also face the challenge of changing business practices. Investment in talent therefore should have equal focus both on meeting the present talent needs and future talent needs of the organization. I have seen in Durgapur Steel Plant, a public sector steel manufacturing unit under Steel Authority of India (SAIL), is currently investing in building talent for future new technology operations to avoid any time-lag and the performance setback.

In addition to above, many organizational practices also suggest mentoring role models, and the need for harnessing the talent pool for utilization of talent potentialities available in the organization, as other important principles for designing talent development programs. As has already been argued in the beginning, we cannot have any universal principles for designing talent development programs, as these are highly situational and organization specific.

Final Take

1. Depending on the nature of talent development program, ROI can be either tracked quickly or after a long gap.
2. Quick ROI tracking is possible for training and learning, when used as a talent development program. When coaching and mentoring are used as talent development tools, tracking ROI is possible only after a long gap.
3. Ethical consideration in talent development stems from organizational talent development policies.
4. Ethical talent development practices, apart from organizational brand building, can attract new talents and enhance employee engagement.
5. Even the positive word of mouth cascades to customer retention and new market development.
6. Principles for designing talent development programs depend on the typical business focus and strategies of an organization.

Talent development in Indian organizations: Lessons from Reliance Industries Limited (RIL)

Talent development is a challenge not only for Indian organizations; it is now a global issue. One of the studies of CIPD (2009) could trace Indian talent shortage is alarming over the years. Top talents migrate to other countries and this requires Indian organizations to come out with some strategies to source top talents globally. CIPD reports observe that Indian organizations' talent development focus is more ad hoc than systemic. Many Indian organizations even today refrain from performing the critical tasks of human resource planning. They prefer recruitment on requirement basis, resulting inability to attract talents for long-term business sustainability. That India is now strong with IT talents is more a myth than reality. Most of the IT majors in India started sourcing their talents globally, including those top Indian talents, who earlier migrated to other countries. A good example of sourcing is Vishal Sikka, present CEO of Infosys, with internationally competitive terms.

(Box continued)

(Box continued)

RIL, during their formative days, had the practice of sourcing talents from public sector enterprises. But today the company has focused on in-house talent development. With employee age-mix of 41 years, the company focus on continuous learning and development reinforcement, powered by their own RALP, that is, Reliance Accelerated Leadership Program. Talent development process in the organizations is further powered by their continuous process development with six-sigma approach, focus on best compensation and branding, new talent acquisition (especially in the age group of 20s and 30s), and continuous HR transformation.

RALP is designed for high-performing professionals in their age group of 27–35, so that they can be developed as strong leadership cadre to supplement the future talent pipeline over a period of 5–10 years. This 104-week RALP is powered by detailed orientation, rotation in different functions and business verticals, including cross-functional, and then leadership training. Rotations, including cross-functional rotations balance the interests of the employees, their experiences, their potential fit for higher level roles in the organization.

Although RALP is for those who perform the best, the company supports others through their continuous learning and development programs, so that such employees can also join the talent pipeline. The culture of innovation, continuous learning, and RALP today could make RIL a talent-driven organization.

Summing Up

This chapter discussed in detail the talent development process in organizations, drawing inputs from theories and organizational practices, including the experiences of the author. Talent is scarce, and organizations across the world have to compete for talent. Hence, organizations have to continuously develop talent pacing with the changing business needs and strategies.

The scope of talent development extends to incubation of in-house talents, and developing the newly hired talents, pacing with the changing needs and strategies of the organizations. Holistic talent development requires developing a talent-driven organization culture. Talent pipeline in organizations has to meet both the present and future talent requirements of the organization.

Talent development plans time to time need to be calibrated with the changing business plans and strategies of the organizations. Talent development process should be business driven, future focused, integrated and capable to deliver measurable results. It is a multi-dimensional activity in the organization, and it requires careful planning.

Aditya Vikram Birla Group—World Class Talent Development

Aditya Birla Group, today a US\$40 billion corporation with headcounts of 120,000 employees. The company has a vibrant presence in many countries of the world, though it has Indian roots. Globally, the company is ranked 4th among top 25 companies of the world for leaders. Such laurels for an Indian multinational company obviously prompt us to study the talent development practices of the company, to draw lessons for other to emulate.

The group acknowledges its commitment to talent emphatically stating with unearthing of iron, copper, bauxite, or manganese, they also unearth talent. Interestingly, believing in omnipresence of talent, the group further demonstrates the inclusive approach to talent development, not just limiting it to privileged few.

After identifying the talent, the group makes use of multiple talent development tools, like classroom training, coaching and participating in special project teams, etc. The idea behind this is to enable employees to continuously learn and develop, and in the process help in building the talent pipeline of the organization. With an institutionalized learning culture, the group envisages both on-the-job and off-the-job learning, sensitizing the students within the talented employees. With such learning thrust, employees learn new skills, acquire new competencies and discover their new ways of doing business.

(Case Study continued)

(Case Study continued)

Learning both on and off the job has now become a way of life for the employees. The group encourages each other to learn new skills, acquire new competencies and discover new ways of doing business.

A successful employer branding, focusing on important milestones of group's growth path, successive acquisitions and expansions, and commitment to capitalize the emerging global market opportunities, legitimately attracts new talents to the organizations. Moreover, new talents get the opportunity to work across different verticals, and even develop them for future cross-functional jobs. With supportive HR practices, employee benefits programs, talented people find the group as one of the best employer, resulting their lifelong bonding with the organization.

This case has been developed from the website inputs of the Group.

Bibliography

Avedon, M. J., & Scholes, G. (2010), Building competitive advantage through integrated talent management. In R. Silzer & B. E. Dowell (Eds), *Strategy-driven talent management: A leadership imperative.* Jossey-Bass, San Francisco, CA, pp. 73–122.

Bhattacharyya, D. K. (2013). *Evidence based strategic human capital management: A study on Durgapur steel plant in strategic approaches for human capital management and development in a turbulent economy.* USA: IGI Global, pp. 53–72.

Cappelli, P. (2008). *Talent on demand: Managing talent in an age of uncertainty.* Boston, MA: Harvard Business Press.

Chartered Institute of Personnel and Development (CIPD). (2009). *The war on talent? Talent management under threat in uncertain times.* London: CIPD.

Conger, J. A. (2010). Developing leadership talent: Delivering on the promise of structured programmes. In R. Silzer & B. E. Dowell (Eds), *Strategy-driven talent management.* San Francisco, CA: Jossey-Bass, pp. 281–312.

Dickmann, M., Brewster, C., & Sparrow, P. R. (Eds). (2011). *International human resource management: Contemporary issues in Europe.* London and New York, NY: Routledge.

Gandz, J. (2006). Talent development: The architecture of a talent pipeline that works. *Ivey Business Journal Online,* January/February, 1–4.

Gladwell, M. (2010). *Outliers: The story of success.* Boston, MA: Little, Brown & Company.

Haskins, Mark E., & Shaffer, George R. (2010). A talent development framework: Tackling the puzzle. *Development and Learning in Organizations, 24*(1), 13–16.

Hearn, G., Roodhouse, S., & Blakey, J. (2007). From value chain to value creating ecology. *International Journal of Cultural Policy, 13*(4), 419–436.

Kaye, B. (2002). *Up is not the only way: A guide to developing workforce talent.* Palo Alto, CA: Consulting Psychologists Press.

Lepak, D. P., & Snell, S. A. (1999). The human resource architecture: Toward a theory of human capital allocation and development. *The Academy of Management Review, 24*(1), 31–48.

McDonnell, A., & Collings, D. G. (2011). The identification and evaluation of talent in MNEs. In H. Scullion & D. G. Collings (Eds), *Global talent management.* London: Routledge, pp. 56–73.

Michaels, E., Handfield-Jones, E., & Axelrod, B. (2001). *The war for talent.* Boston, MA: Harvard Business School Press.

Novations. (2009). *Talent development issues study.* Long Island, NY: Novations Group, pp. 1–20.

Porter, Michael E. (1985). *Competitive advantage.* New York: The Free Press.

Potts, J. (2006). The open society and its generators: Toward an evolutionary analysis of creativity, culture and the economy. ARC Centre of Excellence in Creative Industries and Innovation, QUT Working Paper 2, Brisbane.

Pruis, E. (2011). The five key principles for talent development. *Industrial and Commercial Training, 43*(4), 206–216.

Ready, D. A., Conger, J. A., & Hill, L. A. (2010). Are you a high potential? *Harvard Business Review, 88*(6), 78–84.

Scullion, H., & Collings, D. G. (2011). *Global talent management.* London: Routledge.

Wilson, M. S., & Van Velsor, E. (2011). A new terrain of leadership development: An Indian perspective. In S. Verma (Ed.), *Towards the next orbit: Corporate odyssey.* New Delhi: SAGE.

Wilson, M. S., Van Velsor, E., Chandra, A., & Criswell, C. (2011). *Grooming top leaders: Cultural perspectives from China, India, Singapore and the United States.* Greensboro, NC: Centre for Creative Leadership.

Retaining Talent

Introduction

Apple has a "walled garden" strategy to restrict customers to modify its devices, using competing products and services. This is what IBM did during their initial years to force customers to use their software and hardware for their devices, which they could not sustain in the long run. "Walled garden" strategy is different from "open-plan" strategy or "open-architecture" strategy. "Open-plan" strategy allows the customers to modify their devices after purchase, using others' products and services. Many corporate analysts feel that this is the calculated gamble of Apple to delight customers captivating them.

Like captivating customers, the company has now extended it to executive compensation design to attract and retain a talented, entrepreneurial and creative team of executives who will provide leadership for the company's success in dynamic, competitive markets.

The company seeks to accomplish this goal in alignment with the long-term interests of the company's shareholders. The Compensation Committee oversees the executive compensation program and determines the compensation for the company's executive officers. The company believes the compensation program for the top executive officers is instrumental in helping them achieving good performance results in a competitive market. Top executive officers are expected to contribute as a member of the executive team to the company's overall success rather than merely achieve specific objectives within that officer's area of responsibility. Each top level executive officer is an employee of the company for at least 10 years and none has an

(Box continued)

118

(Box continued)

employment agreement or severance arrangement. The executive compensation program for the executive officers consists of
three elements: long-term equity awards in the form of restricted
stock units (RSUs), annual performance-based cash bonus awards,
and base salaries.

Talent retention is defined as general propensity of talented
employees to continue with their organization for certain specific
talent management practices, like employee engagement, empowerment, career development opportunities, competitive compensation, and rewards, etc. Apart from these, organizations are also
able to retain talent, creating their brand value. So proactive TM
practices, together with increased brand value of the organization,
help in talent retention. Talent retention helps organization to
sustain and grow, avoiding wasteful expenses for talent attrition.
Good organizations develop their specific talent retention strategies, and implement that right from day one of talent acquisition.
For example, when career development opportunities are used as
a tool for talent retention, newly acquired talents are briefed on
this right from day one, so that they can prepare their mindsets for
career aspirations.

Problem of talent retention in organizations across the globe can
be attributed to number of reasons. However, the most promi-
nent ones are poor talent management practices, lack of employee
engagement, absence of people centric work environment and culture, less competitive compensation and rewards, etc. But again
such problems are difficult to identify and even if identified, problems cannot be easily solved. One of the top 25 companies in talent
management, based in India, despite their well-known "future
leadership program," and their commitment to talent development, even observe the problem of retention among talented
middle level managers. Reason they attribute to leave the company
is something astonishing—"our company has already reached to
the level of saturation in growth, hence our job is less challenging."
This Indian company, which is the Indian arm of international

FMCG group, is adjudged as the best performer, even surpassing their international counterparts.

Every organization tries to retain talent, else they get defeated in competition, because talent attrition not only creates the immediate performance problem, but also enhances the cost for new acquisition of talents. Therefore, it is the responsibility of HR managers, so also the top management of the organization, to focus on appropriate TM activities, so that talented people continue feeling satisfied with their job, and with the culture of the organization as a whole. At times organization also fails in promoting the culture of talent retention for typical managerial practices. A talented employee may be perceived as a threat to his/her immediate boss. Hence, the boss may create problem for such talented employee and persuade him/her to leave. In most of the cases, organization will go for the boss, as boss is considered more prudent in managing the employees, but there may be exceptions too. Some organizations are powered by robust exit management systems, and exit interviews are taken by the senior level managerial employees, other than the boss. In such cases, when true reasons for leaving the company are identified, organizations may try their best for alternative accommodation for talented employees. Highly performance driven organization, if required in such cases, even replaces the boss to accommodate the talented employees.

Why Talent Retention Is Important

Apart from these reasons like performance failure and rising cost of talent replacement, talent retention is also important for an organization for number of other reasons. Some of the general reasons are discussed below:

- Process of getting talent replacement may not be easy. In many cases, we find even organizations need to wait for a long time. For example, Apple has to wait for more than a year to get their talent replacement at senior management level.

- Job-fit is not the only answer. We may find talent with perfect job-fit, but that may not solve our problem. Organization and culture-fit are also important. Often talented people may not align with the organization and the culture of the organization, causing their mismatch, defeating the purpose of talent replacement.
- A talent left is a talent added to competitor. Talent movement is very high among the competing organizations, which are in same line of business. Hence for the organizations that are losing talents, are also risking further to lose their competitive strengths, as competitors become more powerful in grabbing such talents.
- Newly acquired talents require time to adjust, and such intervening period is a loss to the company for drop in performance and productivity.
- Loyalty and commitment from the newly acquired talent is not time-tested, hence raise a question mark. Companies may have the risk of losing the both.
- Big talents leave means others follow. It has been experienced by many organizations, including Wipro in India. Hence, take every precaution to stop talent attrition.
- High talent attrition dilutes organizational brand value. When your talents leave, you also dilute your brand value. New talents may be skeptical to join.

This list of talent retention is not exhaustive. Many organizations invest time for talent development, spanning over several years and huge sum of money. For long-drawn coaching and mentoring programs, they put their senior managers and executives. Loss of talent attrition in such organizations is colossal. At times even it is difficult to measure. Cost of talent retention through different proactive talent management programs, and streamlining of organizational culture, are far less that the cost of talent attrition. Therefore, organizations need to have effective talent retention strategies to avoid talent attrition.

Final Take

Talent retention is general propensity of talented employees to continue with their organization for certain specific talent management practices, like employee engagement, empowerment, career development opportunities, competitive compensation, and rewards, etc.

Apart from these, organizations are also able to retain talent, creating their brand value.

Proactive talent management practices, together with increased brand value of the organization, help in talent retention.

Good organizations develop their specific talent retention strategies, and implement that right from day one of talent acquisition.

High talent attrition dilutes organizational brand value. When your talents leave, you also dilute your brand value. New talents may be skeptical to join.

Talent Attrition—Some Theoretical Connotations

Talented employees leave organizations for a number of reasons, which we have covered while explaining the strategies of talent retention. Here we are trying to examine the theoretical connotations of talent attrition. Griffeth and Hom (2001), while examining the types of employee turnover, have classified it into three types—voluntary–involuntary, functional–dysfunctional, and avoidable–unavoidable. We can extend such theoretical arguments for talent attrition as well. Organizational concern is to retain talents, when such attrition is voluntary, avoidable, and dysfunctional in nature. In most of the cases such attrition is initiated by the talented employees, for one reason or the other.

Another important issue of talent attrition is the need for thinking beyond the economic aspect of talent attrition. Talent attrition equally affects the organizational performance as a whole. It may be a deterrent for sales, employees' morale, market image of the organization, etc. For such reasons, Batt (2002) and Huselid (1995) recommended for immediate interventions from organization to reduce the rate of talent attrition. Shaw, Delery, Jenkins, and Gupta (1998), and Shaw, Gupta, and Delery (2005) came out with other interesting observations that with the talent attrition, companies also lose their social capital, as such talented people maintain wide networks of social relationships. Losing social networks for the organization means negative performance impact. Therefore, it is important to have some well-thought strategies for talent retention.

Attracting and retaining top talent—Lessons from Warren Buffett

Michael L. Stallard (2014) based on his analysis of Warren Buffett's strategies for attracting and retaining top talent could identify following lessons from us:

Ignite sense of pride and confidence. This is possible when you trust your people, delegate to them the decision-making power, and do not reprimand them for their honest mistake.

Show respect for your people, giving credit to them for the success of organization. For Buffett, talent has no age for retirement. Many top talents in their eighties still take pride to work with him.

Make yourself approachable and open. Buffett even admits his mistakes, and acknowledges what he learns from his managers. Such approachability and openness make people free in communication with Buffet. Their feelings make them energetic, optimistic, trusting, and cooperative.

With the above three mantras, Buffett is successful in attracting and retaining top talent today.

(Developed based on the inputs collected from http://www.foxbusiness.com/business-leaders/2014/02/27/warren-buffetts-3-practices-that-attract-and-retain-top-talent/)

Final Take

Talent attrition is classified into three types—voluntary–involuntary, functional–dysfunctional, and avoidable–unavoidable.

Organizational concern is to retain talents, when such attrition is voluntary, avoidable, and dysfunctional in nature. In most of the cases such attrition are initiated by the talented employees, for one reason or the other.

Apart from the economic aspect, talent attrition equally affects the organizational performance as a whole.

Employee Engagement and Talent Retention Strategies

Employee engagement denotes employees' sense of belongingness to the organization, which culminates to their passion, excitement, and commitment to work. Primarily loyalty and commitment are the two terms we use to indicate employees' engagement to organization. Loyalty and commitment to the organization are the two determinants which we use to understand the engaged and disengaged employees of any organization. Characteristically, we find engaged employees are more productive and they always feel excited about their jobs. They strive to deliver higher performance results and always remain committed toward their organizations. On the other hand, disengaged employees are lacking in their sense of responsibility, and hence fail in their performance. Such employees are by nature lazy, and propensity to avoid their job.

Your Take—C-suite

What you do in building a robust talent retention strategy

You know talent now plays important role in your organizational success. Hence, it is now important for you to build a robust talent retention strategy. But the question remains how? Try these quick-fix solutions for results.

(Box continued)

(Box continued)

- Be proactive in framing talent retention strategies. This requires you to spontaneously initiate those actions which can promote employee engagement, retention, recognition, and investment in human capital development.
- Align your talent retention strategies to business goals and organizational strategies.
- Make extensive use of big data analytics in framing your talent retention strategies.

Some of the possible line of actions for talent engagement and talent retention are presented below:

- Many research studies indicated that organizations are able to retain talent with effective employee engagement programs. Hence, employee engagement is used as an important talent retention strategy. However, success of employee engagement programs depends on a number of factors, including the type of engagement program selected by the organization. To ensure the success of employee engagement program, organizations also need to test some initial aspect of organizations' processes, systems, and policies. For example, it is important at the outset to revisit the vision, mission, and core values of the organizations. Often employees fail to relate them with the organizational vision, mission, and values, as they find those incompatible with their own espoused vision, mission, and values. Employee engagement programs within an organization also vary with respect to the hierarchical levels. For example, managerial employees may feel better engaged with the organizations when they feel more empowered in decision making, enjoy functional autonomy, better career advancement opportunities, opportunity to acquire new knowledge and skills, etc. Contrarily, non-managerial employees may feel more engaged with competitive rewards and compensation, better interpersonal relations with managers and supervisors, etc. Hence, for effective talent retention, the organization has to design the appropriate employee engagement programs, without however compromising with the organizational values.

Your Take—HR leaders

Keep your employees engaged with challenging goals

Feedback sessions also provide an opportunity to link employees' job objectives to organizational objectives. Doing so helps employees to keep broader objectives in mind, shows that you recognize their value, and encourages commitment.

Including employees in the goal-setting process is a great way to enlighten commitment and engagement. When employees have input, they're more likely to identify with and actively work toward organizational goals.

- Coaching and mentoring can also be used as important employee engagement tool. Empirically it has been tested that executive mentoring not only helps in developing executive capabilities and confidence, but also demonstrate high commitment for achieving the performance results for the organizations. For example, mentoring relationships at IBM supports the strategic objectives and also builds trust establishing cross-country connections across the IBM people. For its global presence IBM's mentoring program emphasizes on virtual learning on just-in-time basis. This is what IBM calls speed mentoring. Speed mentoring at IBM emphasizes on virtual group mentoring to solve specific problems and to share information having relevance for IBM. ONGC in India also emphasizes on extensive mentoring program. ONGC's polices are employee friendly and encourage workers' participation in management. The process is facilitated by informative, consultative, associative and administrative forum that encourage participation and foster innovative culture. Also, such practices, including the mentoring program, could facilitate in building a positive work environment to propel excellence in ONGC's performance.

- Assign talented employees more challenging work. Talented employees feel suffocated once they realize they have outdated their skills and knowledge, as their present job is less challenging. It is the responsibility of the managers to reassign more challenging jobs to the talented employees, so that they feel more excited and the sense of challenge.
- Good interpersonal relations are a precursor for talent retention. Interpersonal relations not only develop within the job, they also develop through activities outside the organization. Ensure such social gatherings, get-together, considering organization as a family. Inside the organization promote more teamwork, quality circles, cross-functional meetings, etc.
- Draw employee recognition programs, even to celebrate small wins. Some recognition programs may be pre-announced, as part of structured policy guidelines, while some others may be a surprise. Recognition and rewards sensitize people better.
- Ensure performance feedback to the employees, more with a helping node, so that employees feel encouraged to develop. Performance feedback with a negative node demotivates, and talented employees do not enjoy a "feel good" environment. Performance management systems in organizations should be used more as a development tool.
- Ensure compensation and benefits program emphasize more on pay equity. Variables must be based on performance and traceable, as per the pre-announced plans and programs of the organization. It is important to understand in Indian culture pay equity is more valued that pay inequity, that is, differential pay on extreme merit basis. But it does not mean Indian organizations do not believe in performance-related-pay (PRP), we have PRP, but it represents a small fraction of total compensation and benefits. Designing compensation and benefits strategies in discussions with the employees of the organization, significantly motivates them and in the process helps in talent retention.
- Ensure that employee-related policies, rules, etc., are reasonable and employee friendly. When talented employees find

such policies and rules are oppressive, they decide to quit the organizations.

- Many researches indicate we do not have any universal talent retention strategy. Organizations have to frame their own strategy, duly understanding their nature of problems in talent retention. While exit interview is the final check point, time-to-time organizational diagnosis can help us in understanding the problems of talent retention, and accordingly help us to come out with some effective change in our systems, practices, and policies, so that such problems can be resolved. Only with competitive compensation and benefits it may not be possible to retain the talent. Streamlining the internal system would be necessary, so that talented employees get the "feel-good" experiences. However, meaningful work, flexi-timing, diversity neutrality, excellent onboarding experiences are some of my important practicing examples of talent retention.

Thus, talent retention requires organizations to adopt multi-pronged strategies, depending on the nature of talent, and level of their jobs. Top-level leadership of the organizations plays the crucial role in framing talent retention strategies, and also monitoring the retention data. Time-to-time policies, systems, and strategies of talent retention are changed to align with the changing business situation, and changing pattern of talent requirements.

Final Take

Employee engagement denotes employees' sense of belongingness to the organization, which culminates to their passion, excitement, and commitment to work.

Loyalty and commitment to the organization are the two determinants which we use to understand the engaged and disengaged employees of any organization.

Employee engagement is used as an important talent retention strategy.

(Box continued)

(Box continued)

> Employee engagement programs within an organization also vary with respect to the hierarchical levels.
>
> Coaching and mentoring can be used as important employee engagement tool.
>
> Challenging work, good interpersonal relations, employee recognition programs, performance feedback to employees, equity in compensation and benefits programs and reasonableness in employee related policies, etc., can enhance employee engagement and consequent employee retention.
>
> Effective talent retention requires organizations to adopt multi-pronged strategies, depending on the nature of talent, and level of their jobs.

Motivation as Key Talent Retainer

Many international level studies could come out with the results that when motivation level of employees is very high, they feel engaged, and prefer to continue with the organization with a long-term perspective. This is also relevant for talented people of the organizations. When talented people feel motivated in the organization, their behavior becomes more performance oriented and they try to achieve the best results for the mutual interest of the organization and themselves. Individual behavior is important for employee motivation. Talented employees of the organizations individually behave to meet their unsatisfied needs in the organization. It is for the organizations to capture such unsatisfied needs, which drive the behavior of individual talents, and come out with some motivational reinforcements. For many talented employees money may not be the prime motivator. Talented employees value more relationships, sense of belongingness, intellectual stimulation, challenging work assignments, opportunity for self-development, etc. Therefore, such motivational reinforcement, in general, may be more important for talent retention. Many research studies indicated that when talented employees feel motivated, they not only perform better and contribute to higher productivity, they also focus on quality improvement, and exert their highest level of efforts to get the work done. Their sense of ownership of their work, and identity with the organizations help in building perennial relationships with the organizations.

Career Planning and Development for Talent Retention

Over the employment life cycle of individual employees he/she gets associated with the series of jobs or work-related activities. Career is defined as succession of such jobs, arranged in hierarchical orders. Talented employees when move through such succession of jobs, we call it career movement. More appropriately career can be defined as an integrated pace of vertical and lateral movement in an occupation of an individual over his/her employment span (Bhattacharyya, 2011). Talented employees expect their quick career succession in their organizations. Hence when organizations fail to offer appropriate career plans and career development opportunities, they lose their talents. Today's organizations, therefore, strategically design their career planning and career development opportunities, so that talented employees can make their informed decision to continue their employment with the organization, thus benefitting the organization with talent retention.

Thus, career is vertical or lateral movement of talented employees through sequence of jobs, accompanied by increased responsibilities, status, power, achievements, and benefits. Career plans are documented career progression paths, and career development are opportunities created by the organizations to develop the talented employees, so that they can rise through the career ladder. Increased career development opportunities in the organizations mean increased chance of career advancement for talented employees, which undoubtedly increase the retention of talents. Career development is more like guiding through the talented employees to move through different hierarchical positions. Globally we have many organizations, where top-level managerial talents are developed within the organizations for scientific career planning and development opportunities. Such top-level talents were initially recruited at the base level job and position by these organizations. Internationally Intel is a good example. In India we have the examples of Tata, Hindustan Unilever, Wipro, etc. Effective career planning and development requires professional career management functions, which incorporate recruitment, onboarding, performance management functions. These also form the part of talent management functions of the organizations. Poor career development opportunities in the organization not only create the talent retention problem, but also significantly reduce the performance levels, and consequent loss of productivity for the organization.

For talent retention, it is important to first understand the career stages in relation to the age group of employees when organizations design their career development programs. Talented employees with exploratory stage of their career (mostly new recruits for the organizations) are difficult to retain, and in fact their rate of attrition is very high. For such new talents it is better to focus them to some specific job with more functional autonomy. In some organizations, such newly recruited talents are compulsorily taken through some job rotation programs, so that they can make their choice of selecting the jobs they like most. Some organizations also recruit talents at middle and senior levels, mostly from their competing organizations. For such newly acquired talents, organizations need to design their career development programs in such a way, so that these people enjoy the sense of accomplishment while doing their jobs. It means job assignments should carry some meaning to them. They must identify with the job. These people are mostly in their establishment or maintenance age groups, hence will be choosing their career movement to those organizations which are prepared to value their talents.

For meaningful career planning and career development programs, organizations need to develop first the skill inventories with all important information about the employees, like performance record and rations, inter-personal competence, strengths and weaknesses, etc. Such skill inventories can thereafter be upgraded to a talent pipeline, so that organizations can ensure availability of talents both for meeting the present and future requirements. Career planning and development programs need to the strengthened with training, systematic review and counseling, etc. Only then organizations can ensure availability of the right talent, at right place, and right time.

Succession Planning

Growth and survival of the organization are the responsibilities of the top management. To fulfill such responsibilities each organization needs to plan management succession. Succession planning is done in different time frames to ensure the availability of right managerial personnel at the right time in right positions for continuing organizational vitality and strength. Most of the organizations plan for immediate requirements matching with their budgets and business plans. This short sightedness leads them to an alarming situation, when they find shortage of managerial manpower to man different positions in the organization, resulting to organizational collapse. To avoid this, good organizations try to make succession planning in three different time frames, that is, immediate (within one year), intermediate (one to five years), and long-range (beyond five years). Prevailing managerial attitude, that is, a potential threat from successor, which may not sustain the desire of the managers to cling to their chairs, also stands against the success of the succession planning.

Steps of Succession Planning

The first step is to prepare and develop a management staffing plan for all anticipated needs in different time frames. For important positions at the top managerial level, such planning should be done even for shorter duration, keeping in view the potential threat from eventual natural wastages (death, disability, premature retirement, etc.) and so also from job switch and change (which has now increased many times for obviously enhanced scope of job mobility). Other effects of external factors like economic factors, overall manpower factors should also be considered while making such plan.

Each organization has to review their business plans. Effects of such plans on managerial needs also need to be studied.

The second step is staffing and development. Staffing is concerned with recruitment, selection, and placement. Selection and placement may be either done from outside or from within the organization through promotion and transfer. Development of managerial personnel is done through training, job rotation, creating "Assistant-to" positions, projects, and boards assignments, performance appraisal, counseling and guidance. In many organizations, management adopts what they call grooming process for filling up important managerial positions. A manager is "groomed" by giving temporary assignments, attaching him/her with the higher officer or sometimes designating the potential promotee as "officer on special duty."

The third step is to ensure congenial organizational environment to retain the desired managerial personnel. Unless this is done, the whole exercise of developing a successor may have to be repeated. The fourth step is to develop a good performance appraisal system to get feedback on managerial performance and to review their progress and shortfalls.

Preparation of Management Resource Inventory is the final step in the succession planning. Such Inventory contains details of personal data, performance records, skills, potential, career goals, and career paths of managerial personnel. To make the succession planning process effective, it is important to strengthen it through management development programs. It is a scientific training process for managers and executives to enrich their knowledge and skills, so as to make them competent to manage their organizations effectively. Unlike general purpose training, management development programs aim at developing conceptual and human skills of managers and executives through organized and systematic procedure. Apart from training, management development programs in organizations also make extensive use of job rotation, creation of assistant-to-position, assignment of identified successors to various boards and projects, etc. Finally, organizations also undertake the strategy of organizational development to bring about planned changes from the top for developing the future managers.

Best practices in succession management

Effective succession planning and management not only works as most useful talent retention tool, it also helps organizations for building the talent pipeline. Incubating future leaders from within is still practiced by many organizations. Dell Computer believes in aligning their succession management programs with the core strategies of the organization. CEO of the company collaborates with the succession team, so that talent pipeline is maintained in the organization or ensuring the present and future talent flow. Similarly at Dow Chemical, CEO gets actively involved in succession management for talent flow in the organization. Interestingly for succession management, companies are not always over reliant with big data or talent analytics alone. Dell believes in continuous adjustment of the succession management systems, based on the feedback from the line managers. Such feedback is analyzed in the context of big data and benchmarked information from the top class organizations, for bringing change in the succession planning and management systems.

Final Take

When talented people feel motivated in the organization, their behavior becomes more performance oriented and they try to achieve the best results for the mutual interest of the organization and themselves.

Talented employees expect their quick career succession in their organizations. Hence, when organizations fail to offer appropriate career plans and career development opportunities, they lose their talents.

Effective career planning and development requires professional career management functions, which incorporates recruitment, onboarding, and performance management functions. These also form the part of talent management functions of the organizations.

Succession planning is done in different time frames to ensure the availability of right managerial personnel at the right time in right positions for continuing organizational vitality and strength.

Effective succession planning and management not only work as most useful talent retention tool, it also helps organizations for building the talent pipeline. Incubating future leaders from within is still practiced by many organizations.

Valuing Diversity as Talent Retention Strategy

Among other factors, globalization has now made workforce diversity a natural phenomenon in every organization, irrespective of their national and international operation. Organizations which are operating in national boundary equally face diversity issues in terms of culture, caste, gender, religion, language, etc. Managing workforce diversity in any organization, national or international, requires strict adherence to the principles of uniformity. Workforce diversity, per se is not bad for the organizations. Globally, we have examples of many successful organizations, which could achieve competitiveness, pooling the collective efforts of diverse workforce. Also, we have evidence from many global organizations which could become more innovative for their workforce diversity. Hence, it is important for organizations to promote workforce diversity with an inclusive approach, which at the outset requires creation of level playing field for the minority section of workers, and then create a diversity neutral culture, to leverage the talent and potentiality of diverse workforce. To create diversity-inclusive and diversity-neutral workplace, organizations need to value diversity, embedding with their various HRM practices. Mere adherence to the diversity neutral practices for regulatory compliance is not the answer. It requires careful integration of competing interests of diverse workforce. Without this workforce, diversity may be counter-productive with the increase of conflict, inter-group rivalry, etc. This is evident in most of the public sector companies in India, where workforce diversity practices are followed for regulatory norms than as part of their integrated work culture. Diversity dividend are now well established internationally, without it organizations are more likely to become ineffective and stagnant. In organization diversity issues need to be managed to reap the advantage of innovation, productivity, and performance. This can be observed in case of HP, which rigorously follows the principles of inclusive diversity. HP is one of the forerunners in practicing workplace diversity, which they have started in 1990s. Without diversity, organizations can only survive in the short run, but with diversity organizations can perpetuate its existence. Evidently organizations which are effective in managing workplace diversity are more successful in talent retention. Again excellence in workplace diversity alone is not enough for talent retention. For example HP which values diversity follows the principles of equity, often risks losing of talents. HP observers attribute this to HP's slow response to meritocracy, performance excellence.

The cross-generational work force (veterans, baby boomers, generation X, and generation Y) in same organizations also become important diversity issues, for difference in their values and expectations. In succession planning section, we have discussed this issue partly by raising the age-group factor for succession plans. Similarly gender diversity trend is also now evident globally. Throughout the world we find that women are now joining the workforce in increasing numbers. Remote working through telecommunicating is also another important area for workplace diversity. Organizations are now operating in a global scale with their network structure. Obviously all these require our thoughtful diversity management practices, again putting in our mind the prime need for talent retention.

For international movement of talents, cultural diversity is also now recognized as important workplace diversity issue. Expatriate talent retention nowadays valuing cultural diversity has become a major concern, particularly for organizations operating globally. Hence, organizations must respect cultural diversity through broadmindedness, discussions, and cooperation. This requires creation of a climate of mutual trust, understanding, creating a climate of mutual trust and understanding, solidarity to other culture group, and by developing intercultural exchanges, etc. Without cultural diversity, organizations also face the risk of talent attrition.

Even the diversity issues are evident when organizations try to manage their international operations with an ethnographic managerial outlook. Such ethnocentricity created problem for many Japanese organizations for managing their operations in international work sites, including India. We all know the case of Mazda's withdrawal from the United States, even though they were the first automobile manufacturer of Japan who went to the United States.

Some multinationals solve this problem by building their local managerial talents. For example, Coca-Cola manages their local managerial talents with international outlook. In Coca-Cola headquarters at Atlanta, they train their management interns from different developing countries, including India and China for a period of 12 to 18 months, before they are sent back to their respective countries of origin. Such local managerial talents with global view then manage the global business units (GBUs) of the company successfully.

Final Take

Managing workforce diversity in any organization, national or international, requires strict adherence to the principles of uniformity.

With workforce diversity organizations can achieve competitiveness, and become innovative.

To create diversity inclusive and diversity neutral workplace, organizations need to value diversity, embedding with their various human resource management practices.

The cross-generational work force (veterans, baby boomers, generation X, and generation Y) in same organizations also becomes important diversity issues, for difference in their values and expectations.

For international movement of talents, cultural diversity is also now recognized as important workplace diversity issue. Expatriate talent retention nowadays, valuing cultural diversity has become a major concern, particularly for organizations operating globally.

Performance Management Systems (PMS) and Talent Retention

Effective PMS also helps in talent retention. Effective PMS can track excellent performers and can further nurture their talent using various human resource development programs. Career development is in fact facilitating the employees to rise through the ladders, acquiring higher skills and knowledge. Through succession plans, organization can identify the successors for future managerial positions, and can accordingly develop them through various human resource development initiatives. In all these cases, PMS plays the most crucial role, as it systematically tracks the potentiality of people and accordingly can develop them so that organizations can sustain competitiveness with the best possible human resources.

Retention of talents is an important strategic issue for organizations. Retention is best ensured with a transparent career planning and development initiative. Similarly for internal manning of managerial talents, organizations should also have appropriate succession planning, or else this may jeopardize organizational plans. Succession planning succeeds management development and organizational development. Finally, PMS in organizations reinforces career planning, career development, and succession planning.

Performance Counseling

This is also another talent retention tool. It is a process of advising an employee, listening to his/her problems and enabling him/her to find a satisfactory solution on his/her own. Performance counseling is a process to help subordinates to analyze their performance objectively. It helps in identifying training and development needs and also ensures improvement in future performance of an employee. In this process, it is also used as an effective talent retention tool.

To understand how performance counseling helps in talent retention, we need to first document how it extends help to employees in the organizations. Some of the organizational experiences on performance counseling are as under:

- Helping employees to understand their strengths and weaknesses.
- Giving feedback information about the employees' behavior, so also their performance, which help in improving professional and interpersonal competence.

- Helping employees in setting goals and formulating action plans.
- Helping employees to identify different alternatives for dealing with problems.
- Encouraging employees to feel encouraged to openly discuss their aspirations, conflicts and problems.

With the help in performance counseling process, organizations facilitate in supporting talent development and retention, as employees get the feeling of supportive work environment. However, effectiveness of performance counseling depends on the climate of mutual trust, confidence, openness, free participation of employees' in the review process, focus on employee development, etc.

Role of Organizational Development as Important Talent Retention Strategy

Organization development (OD) is a holistic process of changing both the people and the organizations for overall growth. It involves bundle of people development activities, right from career planning, career development, leadership development, team building training, organizational diagnosis and development, management of change, human capital management, performance management, knowledge management, coaching, and mentoring, etc. In fact, all the areas of HRD activities help in OD. It is not that every organization has to perform all the HRD activities for OD. In some of the areas, they may have already achieved the excellence. Organizations need to narrow their focus, depending on their appropriate areas of intervention, which they identify through diagnosis. For diagnosis, we have many survey tools, each of which can provide us some meaningful insights on current situation of organization, therefore, in the process, can help us in diagnosis.

Through OD, organizations bring positive changes in the work environment and such positive work environment bring self-fulfilling work culture for talented employees. As a result their "feel good" experiences enhance, and they continue with their organizations. Therefore, OD is not just bringing change in the work environment, OD can also be used as an important talent retention strategy.

However, OD must not be confused with the term management development. Management development is development of managers. Management development, therefore, is concerned with upgrading of managers' skills and abilities, whereas OD, though includes management development, is primarily concerned with improving the total system consisting the organization. Like OD, management development also helps in talents' retention.

Rewards as Strategic Talent Retention Tool

Since the global recession of 2008, organizations are struggling to come out with some reward strategies, which can reduce the cost of compensation, and at the same time can retain the talent. More monetary rewards, as option is losing its significance, as it may weaken the cost competitiveness of the organizations. Globally, organizations are experimenting with non-monetary rewards to increase employee engagement and talent retention. Hay Group based on their study on 230 companies in 20 countries, during 2010, could come out with the "changing face of reward." Globally, organizations are now struggling to institutionalize performance-related pay (PRP) aligning rewards with the performance, differentiating reward for "mission critical" job roles, etc. Now, the group observes reward as a top management issue. Top management considers effectiveness of rewards cost, in terms of incremental change in performance and overall return on investment. Also, effect of tax and other regulatory issues on rewards program are now being considered. For organizations, across the globe, designing cost-effective, performance-driven rewards for the talented employees is therefore an ongoing challenge.

Rewards and recognition (R&R) has a rich history. We find R&R practices in different civilizations, including India

(Bhattacharyya, 2013). That R&R can bring positive change in workers' behavior was also observed in history. Couple of reward components are non-material in nature, like career opportunities, work–life balancing, enabling work culture etc. In designing total reward package, organizations consider these aspects, particularly for managerial talents. R&R is increasingly becoming strategically relevant for organizations to achieve results, which also consider talent retention, among others.

Researchers like Lawler (1990), Schuster and Zingheim (1992) argued that organizations can elicit desired behavior from their employees through effective reward strategy. In framing the reward strategy, Lawler (1995) had recommended the consideration of reward elements, like values that strengthen the reward strategy, reward structures, and reward processes. In crafting a reward strategy to elicit desired behavior from the employees, it is necessary for the organization to understand at the outset, what they intend to change, and what is the basis for such change. Once this is clear, organization can chalk out the desired behavioral constructs from their employees, and can effectively retain talent.

Final Take

Effective performance management systems (PMS) help in talent retention, tracking excellent performers, and further developing them through various talent development programs.

PMS can also strengthen the career development and succession planning programs of the organizations.

Performance counseling is a process to help employees to analyze their performance objectively. It helps in identification of the development needs, giving feedback information, and guiding employees in setting goals and formulating action plans.

For its development focus, performance counseling can also be an effective retention tool.

Organization development (OD) initiatives by bringing positive changes in the work environment, make talented people happy, and in the process increase their retention with the organization.

(Box continued)

(Box continued)

Compensation and rewards programs are also used as strategic talent retention tool. Indian organizations make a balance between the fixed and variable pay introducing performance-related-pay (PRP). Even after maintaining equity talent is recognized through PRP, ensuring their retention.

Why TCS needs to relook into their talent retention strategies

With a mission to help customers to achieve their business objectives with innovative, best-in-class consulting, IT solutions and services, TCS has committed to make their workplace a joy for all stakeholders. With its beginning in 1968 (under Tata Sons Limited), and thereafter incorporation as a separate company in 1995, the company has now grown to US$13.4 billion with headcounts of 300,000. All the espoused values of the organization are focused on talent retention. Such values are: leading change, integrity, and respect for the individual, excellence, learning and sharing. With innovation labs and co-innovation network, TCS could successfully transform their workplace for talent retention. Workplace innovation makes the employees' job more challenging, and this helps in talent retention, even at times when compensation and benefits are not meeting the expectation. This apart TCS focuses on talent engagement through job rotation (matching with the competency), and career discussions. With opportunity to work in different countries for employees, the company today feels more effective in retaining talent, which cascaded to significant drop in their rate of talent attrition. However, not everything in talent management practices is okay in TCS. Systematic phasing out of manpower in TCS on grounds of non-performance or failure to specialize often raises question why the company still pursue their exclusive strategy on talent management. Such involuntary attrition often calls for the need to rethink their talent retention strategies

---

Contemporary Approaches to Talent Retention

Contemporary research studies on talent retention also focus on some important issues, like organizational justice, ambidexterity or ambidextrous human resource management practices, etc. Organizational justice concepts have been pioneered by Greenberg (1990) and Cropanzano (1993). Many subsequent researches also emphasized on its importance for talent retention. Organizational justice means ethical treatment to employees, that is, just and fair human resource management practices. Cropanzano and Greenberg (1997) further said that the concept of justice from the perspectives of the employees of the organization. We have two types of organizational justice: distributive and procedural. The concept of distributive justice is embedded in the famous equity theory of Adams (1963, 1965). As per this theory employees compare their input output ratio with peers to ascertain whether they have been treated fairly or not. A talented employee when finds that he/she has not been fairly treated in giving incentives and rewards, will obviously feel depressed, and may endeavor for next possible chance for job shift, creating the problem of talent retention. Procedural justice on the other hand refers to organizational procedures or process for resource allocation and important human resource management decisions (say compensation design, promotions, performance evaluation, etc.), which the employees may feel discriminatory. These two aspects we are not discussing in detail, but we are making this point clear that organizational justice could be a major issue for talent retention problem in organizations. However, ambidexterity issues or ambidextrous human resource management practices have been discussed in detail, including citing the case of ONGC, the POL conglomerate under public sector enterprises.

Talent Retention through Ambidextrous HR Practices

Ambidexterity is the ability of people to efficiently use both hands simultaneously. Metaphorically, we call it organizational ability to exploit and explore. Ambidextrous organizations are capable of balanced learning through internal practices, sharing the available knowledge (exploitation) and exploring new knowledge, process variation and planned experimentation (Baum, Li, & Usher, 2000;

Levinthal & March, 1993; March, 1991). Ambidexterity or ambidextrous HR practices can also be effectively used for talent retention (Bhattacharyya, 2014). Ambidexterity from HRM perspectives covers HRM practices like organizational structure and design, learning, innovation, and strategies. Again structure and the other constructs of ambidexterity need to be viewed from two different perspectives. Structural ambidexterity requires creation of activity-based structures. Contextual ambidexterity (learning, innovation, and strategies), on the other hand, focuses on managing day-to-day activities, making choices between alignment and adaptation. Gibson and Birkinshaw (2004) could identify four behavioral syndromes of employees of ambidextrous organizations. Such employees prefer to take actions even outside the scope of their job for the broader interests of the organization. They are more motivated and informed for spontaneous action. They adopt new opportunities in alignment with the business strategy, and finally they show dual capacity for alignment and adaptability. Ambidextrous organizations, therefore, align their day-to-day activities with innovation, pacing with environmental changes. Various literature support indicates that ambidextrous organizations, and so also ambidextrous HR practices encompass areas like organizational learning, technological innovation, organizational adaptation, strategic management, and organizational design. Through the analysis of ONGC's ambidextrous HR practices, let us understand how such practices could help ONGC in talent retention.

ONGC's journey to ambidexterity started in the first quarter of 1997, when the company embraced the Asset Based Model of organization structure, in line with the suggestion of Mckinsey & Co. It took ONGC almost four years to institutionalize asset-based model, restructuring the organizations to seven directorates, like Director (Offshore), Director (Onshore), Director (Technology and Field Services), Director (Human Resources), Director (Finance), Director (Exploration), and Director (Corporate Services). To support the asset-based model of organizational structure, the

(Box continued)

(Box continued)

company also made their performance management systems a negotiated contract with quantified targets for each asset head. Full empowerment to each asset head, reengineered supportive HR policies, systems, and practices with this structure helped the company to successfully become ambidextrous. With simultaneous focus on exploratory and exploitative activities, reinforced by proactive HR practices, ambidextrous ONGC emerging as a world-class organization. ONGC was formed in 1959 by an Act of the Indian Parliament. In 1994, ONGC has become a corporate body. Today ONGC is considered to be one of the largest companies in the world in terms of reserves and production in integrated energy business.

ONGC truly reflects the aura of ambidexterity. The ambidextrous HRM practices of ONGC can be understood, reviewing their current HRM practices which support both the exploratory and exploitative initiatives of the company. The first reflection of supportive HRM practices to facilitate ambidexterity is on ONGC's manpower sourcing method. The prime objective of human resource planning of the company is to create a future talent pool for leadership roles. While operational manpower planning is based on the company's work plans and targets, pacing with the technology impacts and changing skill and competency requirements, ONGC constantly source manpower with high individual human capital value, for its transformational (future knowledge based skill and competencies) and operational needs. Operational manpower requirement at the non-executive level (such as graduate engineer trainees, technical and non-technical staff members, etc.) is done assessing the gap between available and required manpower. For low-skill operational jobs, ONGC has the system of manpower outsourcing from their vetted manpower vendors. For transformational manpower planning, ONGC plans for manpower for senior, middle, and junior management level and also for junior executives and staff level positions. Both for operational and transformational manpower, in-house availability is first assessed. For active job rotation policy, ONGC annually restructure their manpower and redeploy their employees, based on unit level requirement. For differences in the nature of manpower requirement, manpower planning is done not only on the demand of the user departments, but also on the assessment of the top manageme nt, considering the age-mix, future demand and the headcounts.

(Box continued)

(Box continued)

> Human Resource Information System (HRIS) of ONGC facilitates human resource capital valuation from manpower inventory data, which the company reports in their annual reports. Recruitment and selection decisions are left to the Asset Centers after initial approval of manpower plan by the competent authority (which for ONGC is the top management). Asset center heads initiate recruitment process and select the source of sourcing, depending on the nature of manpower. A well-structured generic competency model of the company, apart from assessing the skill and domain expertise, is used as recruitment criteria by the company, to ensure the recruited manpower fits to the needs of ambidexterity.
>
> Incentivization for good work plays a crucial role, for motivating and retaining the talent. Despite being a public sector enterprise (usually constrained for pay equality) the company introduced PRP, aligning with individual and company performance. The rate of PRP varies from 40 to 200 percent of base pay depending on the level of employees. More weightage is given for company's performance, making the organization a perfect example of institutionalized team work culture. Again PRP component is rationalized, distributing the weight between profit and incremental profit to make the employees strive for continuous performance improvement.
>
> The HRIS also facilitates ambidextrous HR practices in terms of ROI for training, developing road map for research and development through skill mapping, succession planning, etc. Depending on the criticality of manpower requirements and non-availability of right manpower for regular employment, the company also recruits on tenure-track basis (usually those who are above the age bracket for regular employment requirement). Multi-skilling of employees is done through in-house training. The individual employee values, across all levels to the company now stands at US$2.7 million, and this value showing a consistent trend of increase over the years. Across all the categories, employees in the age-group of 41–50 are having the highest human capital value.
>
> Further to support ambidexterity, ONGC has also taken many other HR initiatives, like use of assessment development center approach for employee development and assessment, employee surveys, business games, team games, coaching and mentoring, etc. All these have been focused on building in-house capabilities.

(Box continued)

(Box continued)

Assessment development center helps the company to identify potential executives for future leadership positions, career progression, identification of competency gap, and for succession planning. The company at present hires about 300 executives per year through assessment development center programs, and uses the results for various HR decisions related to its employees' and organizational development. Employee surveys help the company to map the organizational climate and develop action plans for employee engagement. Business games sharpen the decision-making abilities of managers. Team games evoke cross-functional team spirit among executives and non-executives and understanding of the group dynamics. Coaching and mentoring programs focus on developing 900 coach and mentors every year to increase human resource value of employees, across the various levels of organization.

To further strengthen the ambidextrous HRM practices, ONGC has designed and implemented a job rotation and transfer policy, not just to facilitate inter-organizational movement of employees but also developing their multidimensional knowledge and skills, so that they can choose their own career plan and flexible enough to pursue specialist tracks. Such policies are enforced systematically among all employees, and have been made as essential criteria for promotion. With delegation of power, up to E-4 (Senior Executives) level, executives' transfer decisions are vested with asset center's level. Such delegation significantly empowers unit heads to restructure and redeploy manpower with flexibility to meet the needs of ambidextrous organizations.

A bundle of welfare measures for employees of ONGC in the form of soft-interest loans, medical facilities, social security schemes, post-retirement benefit scheme, etc., made the organization the most employee friendly, and among others impacted on the high rate of retention. To recognize the talents, company has also instituted number of awards scheme, pacing with the strategic needs. Awards are based on the outstanding performance, creativity, organizational abilities, teamwork, etc., to encourage service excellence.

To continuously develop the human capital, ONGC has five specialized training institutes and four regional training institutes. In addition, five dedicated research and development institutes of ONGC also significantly contribute to human capital development through institutionalized innovation culture,

(Box continued)

(Box continued)

both for the current and for the future activities. In the year 2011–2012, the company has invested 172,208 man days for training, averaging to 5.2 man days per employee. ONGC Academy acts as a nodal center for training and development activities of the company. Specialized training institutes focus on training on drilling technology, well control, oceanography and metrology, safety handing of explosives, and radioactive devices in seismic and well logging operations, new generation equipment, oil and gas production and processing, etc. Many national and international organizations also avail the ONGC's training and development support for their employees. Despite strong in-house training and development base, the company also makes use of various nationally and internationally known training partners, including professional bodies, world class organizations, and universities.

The focus on continuous development of employees, making them the right fit for ambidexterity, ONGC had planned for 221 man days of training on exploration related activities, spread across 42 programs in 2012–2013. To leverage world class expertise, 30 such programs had been conducted retaining the services of best organizations across the globe, and 12 are conducted through their internal training set-ups. High focus on management development programs (MDPs) almost 25 percent to total training, and 17.5 percent focus on exploration related training, truly speak about ONGC's emphasis on ambidexterity through development of people, balancing their exploration and exploitation activities. All these ambidextrous HR initiatives have now made ONGC to achieve innovation, and sustainable organizational development through talent retention.

Talent Retention after Merger and Acquisition

Retaining talent after merger and acquisition is one of the most important challenges of the acquiring organizations. Although technology companies are now in their acquisition spree, primarily for talent acquisition from the acquired companies, we see the problem of talent retention in most of these cases. Primary reasons for talent attrition from the acquired companies are fear of subordinate to the peer group members of the acquiring companies, and apparent mismatch with the culture. A Towers Watson study emphasized on the importance of having some clear talent retention strategies in such cases, else acquiring companies may face the flight of talents, at times even defeating the purpose of merger and acquisition (M&A). In M&A we find companies remain busy in other critical business alignment issues, legal issues, etc., as a result talent retention issue gets neglected. But the companies feel the pinch once they find talent attrition from acquired units.

Final Take

Ambidextrous HRM practices provide opportunities to talented employees to simultaneously focus on future innovation and development issues, while they do their present jobs. It requires HR practices, which allow enough free time to employees to pursue their projects (as is done in Google), career by choice (CBC) options (as in HUL), and overall organizational commitment to exploratory activities, balancing their present operation.

Organizations which embrace ambidextrous HR practices, can achieve high talent retention.

As M&A are very common, talented employees in the organizations expect some protective cover, in the event their organizations are acquired by other companies. Golden parachute program, as an age old practice, already exists. But nowadays acquisitions in many cases are for getting talented employees. Acquiring companies make appropriate changes in their systems to accommodate the talents of the acquired organizations. Talent retention in such cases, therefore, depend on the degree of effectiveness of such systems.

Talent retention is compensation + + for ICICI

ICICI Bank, the second largest bank in India, extensively uses their compensation and benefits program as important talent retention strategies. In addition to the employee stock options (ESOPs), the bank this year significantly hiked (20 percent raise) the compensation packages of their top talents to retain. With new banking licences issued by the Reserve Bank of India (RBI)

(Box continued)

(Box continued)

the bank now fears flight of talents, unless compensation packages are designed more and more attractively. Many critics feel this cannot be a sustainable talent retention strategy. Despite high compensation packages, ICICI faces the problem of talent retention, though its magnitude is within the limit.

Like other talent-driven organizations, ICICI Bank also provides the sense of purpose to its employees. With such shared vision, the young talents feel motivated, and actively engage them in the organizational growth. With opportunity to learn and grow, empowerment, cross-functional movement, the bank is able to drive the growth retention of talents. But for millennial talents, job movement is a natural syndrome. ICICI constantly innovate and focus on building new skills of their employees, so that millennial talents feel more and more engaged with the organizations.

Summing Up

This chapter highlighted various talent retention strategies for the organizations.

Talent retention is general propensity of talented employees to continue with their organization for certain specific talent management practices, like employee engagement, empowerment, career development opportunities, competitive compensation and rewards, and for high brand value of the organization.

Good organizations develop their specific talent retention strategies, and implement that right from day one of talent acquisition. Employee engagement is used as an important talent retention strategy. Effective career planning and development, and succession planning programs in the organizations also help in talent retention. Similarly valuing workforce diversity, adopting effective performance management systems (PMS), balancing compensation and rewards programs, and by systematic organizational development (OD), organizations can ensure talent retention.

Ambidextrous HRM practices provide opportunities to talented employees to simultaneously focus on future innovation and development issues, while they do their present jobs. It can also help in talent retention. In mergers and acquisitions, organizations need to take necessary steps to ensure talents of the acquired units are retained.

Why Talent Retention Is a Challenge: Story of DuPont

Without any robust talent retention strategies, you cannot retain your people who deliver. Talent retention in DuPont cannot be attributed to their diversity and inclusive compensation and benefits program alone. Rather it is possible for the company to retain talent for their strategic focus on TM practices.

DuPont, the chemical giant, based in the United States was founded in July 1802. With more than two-century legacy, the company today proclaims that they make a difference in everyday life of their employees. To retain talent, the company offers all possible opportunities, so that talented people can make use of their professional and interpersonal skills in the company, and can co-create a talent driven organization.

Talent-driven business focus starts at DuPont right from the acquisition process of HR. The company emphasizes on professionals who aspire to reach to a leading edge of their career, developing future technologies, and pursuing excellence. They call it acquiring those who look for a purpose, and not just a job. Talent acquisition is a four-stage process, identifying, assessing, interviewing, and hiring, so that company can get the best talents.

With talent acquisition the company then ensures talent retention with their very own strategies, like diversity inclusive compensation and benefits program; focusing on total well-being of employees, employee assistance program, pro-family practices, flexible work practices, pro-family benefits, etc. All these no doubt reflect DuPont's master strategy, that is, diversity and inclusion.

Company's commitment to talent retention is evident from the recent proclamation of CEO Ellen Kullman that

(Case Study continued)

(Case Study continued)

"Investment in long-term innovation isn't a burden, it's an asset. Hence for DuPont talent retention is also achieved through building the infrastructure of innovation ecosystems. From a chemical, the company has now transformed to a science company." With the tag line of "Together, we can make the world a better place," further reaffirms company's commitment for talent retention.

With legacy of more than two centuries, the company today operates in more than 90 countries, powered by 150 research and development centers, and 70,000 employees.

Bibliography

Adams, J. S. (1963). Towards an understanding of inequality. *Journal of Abnormal and Normal Social Psychology, 67*, 422–436.

———. (1965). Inequality in social exchange. In L. Berkowitz (Ed.), *Advances in experimental psychology*. New York, NY: Academic Press, pp. 267–299.

Batt, R. (2002). Managing customer services: Human resource practices, quit rates, and sales growth. *Academy of Management Journal, 45*, 587–597.

Baum, J. A. C., Li, S., & Usher, J. M. (2000). Making the next move: How experiential and vicarious learning shape the locations of chains' acquisitions. *Administrative Science Quarterly, 45*(4), 766–801.

Bhattacharyya, D.K. (2011). *Performance management systems and strategies*. New Delhi: Pearson.

———. (2013). R&R are more holistic than C&B: We should rename C&B to R&R. *Compensation & Benefits Review, 45*(5), 286–288.

———. (2014). Sustainable organizational development through innovation and ambidextrous HRM practices: Evidenced based study on ONGC. In F. Soliman (Ed.), *Business innovation and business invention—Leveraging interdependencies for sustainability and organizational development*. USA: IGI Global, pp. 258–275.

Cropanzano, R. (1993). *Justice in the workplace: Approaching equity in human resource management*. Mahwah, NJ: Lawrence Erlbaum Associates.

Cropanzano, R., & Greenberg, J. (1997). Progress in organizational justice: Tunneling though the maze. In C. L. Cooper & I. T. Robertson (Eds), *International review of industrial and organizational psychology*. New York: John Wiley & Sons, pp. 317–372.

Gibson, C. M., & Birkinshaw, J. (2004). The antecedents, consequences, and mediating role of organizational ambidexterity. *Academy of Management Journal*, 47(2), 209–226.

Greenberg, J. (1990). Organizational justice: Yesterday, today, and tomorrow. *Journal of Management*, 16(2), 399–432.

Griffeth, R. W., & Hom, P. W. (2001). *Retaining valued employees*. Thousand Oaks, CA: SAGE.

Huselid, M. (1995). The impact of human resource management on practices, on turnover, productivity, and corporate financial performance. *Academy of Management Journal*, 38, 291–313.

Lawler, E. E. III. (1990). *Strategic pay: Aligning organizational strategies and pay systems*. San Francisco, CA: Jossey-Bass.

———. (1995). The new pay: A strategic approach. *Compensation & Benefits Review*, 27(4), 14–22.

Levinthal, D., & March, J. (1993). Myopia of learning. *Strategic Management Journal*, 14(8), 95–112.

March, J. G. (1991). Exploration and exploitation in organizational learning. *Organization Science*, 2(1), 71–87.

Schuster, J. R., & Zingheim, P. K. (1992). *The new pay: Linking employee and organizational performance*. New York: Lexington Books.

Shaw, J., Delery, J., Jenkins, G., & Gupta, N. (1998). An organization-level analysis of voluntary and involuntary turnover. *Academy of Management Journal*, 41, 511–525.

Shaw, J. D., Gupta, N., & Delery, J. E. (2005). Alternative conceptualizations of the relationship between voluntary turnover and organizational performance. *Academy of Management Journal*, 48, 50–68.

5

Talent Management

Introduction

What makes HUL's talent management (TM) program great?

Hindustan Unilever (HUL), the FMCG major of India with legacy over 80 years, a company which touches the heart of two-third Indians, is another talent-driven organization, globally recognized as 6th out of "25 top companies of the world for leaders." The Aon Hewitt and RM Group research acclaimed many talent development practices of HUL, which are of global standard, and which can be emulated by others as best practice talent development examples.

With Paul Polman, Unilever Plc's CEO's announcement of global strategies for major restructuring of all Unilever's subsidiary across the world, focusing more on austerity measures, like hiving off the products with less than Euro 1 billion annual sales, reducing the stock keeping units (SKUs), etc., we all thought talent development would be Unilever's least priorities across the world. For HUL this was more significant, as the new CEO Sanjiv Mehta, who replaced Nitin Paranjpe, is a man from finance. Apprehension was huge curtailment of middle level managerial jobs, particularly with sales profile, and truncating of talent development activities and other amenities. Speculation was that the job cut may go up to 800 head counts. Undeterred by the restructuring squeezes, with 16,000 strong army, HUL surpassed every speculation and once again they are surged with sales revenue of ₹280,191.3 million.

(Box continued)

(Box continued)

In HUL TM is special, as the focus of the company is always to create great jobs with great responsibilities. It helps the newcomers to get freedom in doing their jobs. With the culture of performance the new comers feel more challenge. The agile work practices, with focus on people recognition, with inclusive HR practices, make HUL the chosen destination for talented employees. What is more interesting, the company provides the opportunity to work flexibly on live projects, under their "career by choice" program. Growth and capability building are again integral part of all cross-sections of employees. The company feels for sustaining in performance capability development is essential for all.

With culture of high performance, HUL ensures clarity of goals in terms of company's expectations from each employee. Employees are helped to track their development in their career progression paths with their individual capability development cards. What is more astounding is company's more concern for performance results than time and attendance. Such flexibility encourages employees, as they enjoy more autonomy and freedom in their work. This is what HUL call "agile workplace."

The TM program of HUL is more holistic, and focused on creating great jobs, inculcating the sense of responsibilities, so that people right from the beginning of their career feel more sensitized about their career and strive for developing in best possible way to become the future leader.

This case has been developed based on the website information of HUL.

Globally organizations are now facing the challenge of competition and sustainability. Operating environment in organizations across the globe is also getting increasingly complex for continuous change in technology and business processes. To manage such complex operating environment, organizations now leverage their talent pool. But talent pool need not represent all cross-sections of employees of the organization, it may consist of those few employees, who are more productive, efficient, and contribute even at exceeded expectations level of performance. With effective TM, organizations can attract, acquire, develop, and retain talents, and institutionalize a talent-driven workplace.

To understand TM, let us first define it from different operational perspectives. TM is a process of individual and organizational development, responding to complex operating environment. Globally operating environment for organizations is changing fast either for technology-induced changes in the process or for intensified competition between organizations for extended market landscape across the world. Effective TM in both the cases can at least help organizations to sustain, if not to grow. Transforming organization to a talent-driven one, it is also possible to grow. This is what we find in world class organizations. Extending this core concept of TM, we can further define it as a process of institutionalizing supportive people-oriented culture in workplaces. Incidentally organizations can foster talent only when work culture is supportive and people oriented.

Considering TM from integrated HRM perspective, we define it as a process of attracting, acquiring, developing, and retaining the right people for the right job at the right time. From this perspective, TM is not only for meeting the present talent needs, but also for the future talent needs of the organizations. In fact what we understand today as TM is an extended human capital management (HCM) approach. Human capital concept per se is a transition from control to commitment approach in HRM literature. Organizations invest in human capital to get incremental change in their business results. Often organizations use the term human capital management interchangeably with TM. TM has to be business aligned, strategy focused in attracting, acquiring, developing, and retaining talent in organizations. As an integrated management process, TM can ensure a robust talent pipeline to make available right people for the right job at the right time. Effective TM can enhance competitive advantage of organization.

More Conceptual Clarity on TM

With these definitions, we can understand the theoretical definitions of TM. But better conceptual clarity on TM is possible when we discuss it with inputs from organizational practices. No doubt before McKinsey's land mark study on "Talent War," for organizations, TM process was like any other administrative functions of HR and limited to potential appraisal to identify talent, developing succession plan, designing exclusive training, and development programs for the fortunate few and thinking on their career development opportunities. Today we see TM as a business-focused strategic activity to develop and maintain the talent pool. Talent value chain now integrates the process of attraction and acquisition of the best-fit for the organization through recruitment, develop such recruits with an inclusive approach, rather than limiting the focus only to those who are outstanding performers, and retain them. Effective TM process can add value at each level of value chain embracing the best practices through innovation, or emulating the world class organizations. Operationally TM therefore is organizational ability to create and use talent to achieve the organizational objectives. It is not just limited to managing technical and managerial talents, rather considering TM more holistically for all cross-sections of people of the organizations. The holistic approach to TM rests on the assumption that people in general have talents, and the onus of the organization is to identify and liberate it.

Realizing the importance of TM, many organizations today make use of automated TM systems. Such automated systems facilitate in talent analytics, and in the process help in critical decision making on TM. However, understanding people is more critical in managing talent, than making use of automated TM systems. Organizations are also embracing TM as knowledge management and human capital management process to bring change. Prima facie there is no conflict with such perceptive thoughts. But for TM it is more important to drive and manage it as a value creating business process. Again value creating potentialities of talent are assessed by organizations differently. For example, 3M considers high value creating potentialities in individual who performs consistently at higher level. Opposed to this approach most of the IT majors in India limit their search for high value creating people in the organizations, matching with their HR plans, that is, the forecasted bench strength. Some international organizations have different benchmark for identifying high value creating people in organizations. They consider those people who can take personal risk in tough situations can really add value. Some Indian companies identify their talents based on internationally benchmarked set of competencies. They consider their people as talented when they observe availability of such competencies in their people.

With the increase in no-poaching settlement with the competing organizations, viz., Adobe, Apple, Google, and Intel are reaching to such settlement; talent sourcing for organizations would be limited to open market source and in-house development. Hence, talent identification process for the organizations needs to address those issues which are appropriate and more business driven. Robust in-house talent identification process, identifying suitable talents, not only helps organization to achieve their business goals but also ensures effective utilization of employees' full potential. Such talent pool can help organizations to further their future plans and programs, including realization of overall business strategy.

Your Take—For HR leaders

Integrate your talent management strategy with organizational strategy

Alignment of TM strategy with organizational strategy requires definition of consistent leadership criteria across all functional areas, and identification of specific competencies (analytical, technical, education, experience) to cultivate for continuing growth. Approach to strategic talent management needs to be more proactive in identification of essential skills requirements, and designing of focused training and development program, designing of job descriptions based on critical skills and competencies requirement for improving the recruitment functions. By aligning TM strategy with the strategies of the organization, an environment of transparency is created, and managers in general and HR managers in particular, can narrow their focus in pursuing the goals, addressing the TM issues, for achieving the overall effectiveness of the organizations.

Even from all these discussions, TM being more a practice-based approach, we may not have any agreed definition. However, we can conceptualize TM by looking at organizational practices.

We can clarify this by citing Lewis and Heckman (2006). According to them TM manifests:

- HR practices or functions which attract, acquire, retain, and develop talent.
- All activities that lead to the creation of a talent pipeline for maintaining talent flow, pacing with the needs of the organization.
- All activities that focus on exclusive or inclusive development of employees.

First two points are now clear from the inputs of previous chapters. The third point has also been discussed in Chapter 3 on talent development. Exclusive approach to employee development limits organization's investment only for identified few who are high performing and who have high potential to grow. Inclusive approach, however, considers all are having talent, and hence taking all through the process of development can significantly build organizational capability and institutionalize a talent-driven work culture.

Final Take

TM is a process of individual and organizational development, responding to complex operating environment.

As an integrated HRM function, primary activities of TM are attracting, acquiring, developing, and retaining right people for the right job at the right time.

Effective TM needs to be business aligned and strategy focused, and effective TM can enhance competitive advantage of the organization.

The holistic approach to TM rests on the assumption that people in general have talents, and the onus of the organization is to identify and liberate it.

Evolution of TM

With the release of McKinsey's path breaking studies "War for Talent," and subsequent changes in the business dynamics, TM has become most strategic and knowledge based role of HRM functions of the organizations. Talent has been recognized as important business differentiator between organizations, and hence managing talent has also enhanced the value adding potentiality of HRM functions. TM, as has already been explained, enables organizations in attracting, developing, and retaining talented people. The scope of talent development also extends to existing employees, who are potential talents for the organizations. Although many organizations across the world always focused on developing their potential employees for future leadership positions through a structured succession planning process, more institutionalized approach in the form of TM is less than two decade old. Despite such importance of TM, many surveys of professional bodies still come out with their warnings that talent or TM process is still neglected in the organizations. Selective in TM approach, limiting it only to identified a few, focus more on TM during economic boom and neglect it during economic recession, more concerned for firm-specific talent development initiatives, etc., are some of the common observations against the organizations. Good or bad is a different debate, because every organization has their strategic priorities and business goals. But what we intend to clarify here that tracing evolutionary process of TM, we do not find any universality in its approach and practices. Even today also we find that organizations differentiate in TM practices.

Evolution of TM is first traced to technology revolution, which is an ongoing process. With globalization, technology transfer is now much easier. Firm's choice for technology upgradation is no longer optional, it is compulsory. Technology alters the skills (for compositional shift), knowledge, and the overall competencies of existing people of the organizations. These alter the talent profile. With technology, business complexities are also increasing day by day, requiring firms to alter their business processes. Thus, change in business processes and change in technology together culminate change in the talent profile of the existing employees both for their present and future jobs. With dried talent pipeline, organizations then look for such talents in new hires.

With alarming note from McKinsey, highly talent-driven organizations are now shifting their TM functions from core HRM functions to the strategic level functions, even at times assigning this role to CEOs. This is evident even in Indian organizations. CEOs of most of the IT majors get them directly involved in TM processes.

From HR perspectives, we can explain the evolutionary process of TM, citing the examples of changing pattern or recruitment functions of the organizations. For example in 1970s, when HR functions was known as personnel management functions, recruitment function was primarily concerned with hiring people, deciding their compensation, and complying with statutory welfare measures. From 1980s onward, with the emergence of strategic HRM functions, recruitment has become not just hiring and compensating and complying with the statutory welfare measures, it extended to recruitment of the right people, developing them, and fitting them with the organization structure. With the emergence of TM, particularly after McKinsey's "War for Talent" study, recruitment now needs to be competency based, must be able to contribute to talent pipeline of the organization, meet the competency gaps, business and strategy aligned. Such process of change in talent acquisition over the years can also guide us to the evolutionary trend in TM.

From TM we have now come to the era of integrated TM. Integrated TM is a process of aligning people to the business goals, values, strategies or the organizations, through a technology enabled a TM system, which facilitates selection, recruitment, rewarding, developing, and retaining the talent in the organizations. Many TM vendors offer integrated TM systems.

Final Take

Evolution of TM is first traced to technology revolution.

With technology, business complexities are also increasing day by day, requiring firms to alter their business processes. Thus change in business processes and change in technology together culminate change in the TM process of the organization.

Need for TM

We have already discussed that TM, whether we consider it as HR function or strategic level function of any organization, is important, as it sources and develops the manpower and makes talent available, pacing with business and strategic needs of the organizations. Organizations by creating their brand identity can attract the talent. Organizational brand building facilitates in communicating value to the prospective talents for the organization, who can make an informed choice by joining the organizations. Therefore, in the process of embracing TM, organizations also develop their brand identity. Increased brand value of the organizations also enhances the goodwill value, and facilitates in increasing the market share. TM therefore even contributes indirectly to business results of the organizations. Direct contribution of TM however reflects through the performance data of employees. Organizations also benefit from TM achieving the business goals. Talented employees by and large deliver at above expectations level of performance.

Traditionally, however, TM functions focus on:

- attraction;
- recruitment;
- development;
- retention;
- potential assessment;
- performance management;
- human resource planning; and
- developing a talent pipeline.

For obvious focus on TM, we also observe, organizations across the globe are also refocusing on their HRM functions. Changing technology and changing global economic environment is increasingly positioning TM functions in top most priorities of HR professionals. Therefore, it is important for the organizations to develop adequate and appropriate plans and put in efforts to attract the best pool of available candidates, and also to nurture and retain the current employees. And to do all these, organizations need effective TM practices.

Some of the important benefits of TM practices, based on organizational experiences are decrease in attrition rate, creating the culture of performance, aligning people with the business and strategies of the organizations. When organizations become talent driven, talented employees prefer to remain in their organizations. Talent-driven organizations also concern themselves with employee development and career progression. Talented employees get the opportunity to learn new things, get the scope to earn competitive pay packets, and enjoy a sense of pride identifying them with the organization.

TM Models

As TM practices widely vary across the organizations, we do not have any general TM model. However, every organization follows certain structured approach in managing talent. For example, simple TM model for any organization could be like Figure 5.1.

Figure 5.1
Talent Management Model

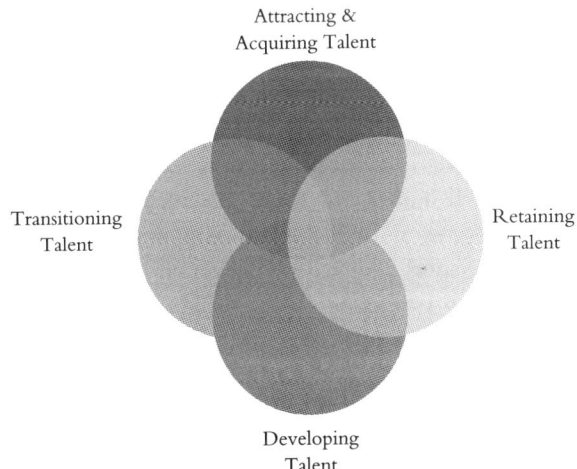

Attracting &
Acquiring Talent

Transitioning
Talent

Retaining
Talent

Developing
Talent

Transitioning talent involves outplacement activities for those who are either redundant or approaching retirement. Rest of the aspects of the above generic TM model have already been discussed earlier.

Among other TM models, Peter Cappelli's talent-on-demand model is mostly referred in TM literatures. Cappelli (2008b) in his famous book *Talent Management for the Twenty First Century*, extending the just-in-time approach of operations and supply chain management, explained this model with four principles. These four principles are as under:

- Make or buy to manage risk.
- Adapt to uncertainty in talent demand.
- Improve return on Investment in developing employees.
- Preserve the Investment by balancing employee-employer interests.

For each principle Cappelli has given adequate justification. For example, organization has to decide on making or buying talent as with a huge number of talented people in the pay roll; organization may not achieve cost efficiency. Similarly adapting to the uncertainty in talent demand, organization can manage the talent demand more effectively. The third principle, that is, improving the ROI in developing employees, gets employees to share in the costs of development. Finally, in our pursuit to preserve the investment, balancing employee-employer interests, we focus on talent development on ongoing basis. The primary lesson from this model, effective TM not only requires organizations to attract the best-fit but also requires focus on nurturing and retaining the current employees. In fact Cappelli's model speaks on core approach to plan, source, develop, and retain in managing talent in organization. It can be explained using Figure 5.2.

As TM focuses on enhancing the potential of people which enhances the capabilities of the organization, basic DNA of the organization lies in the organizational capabilities, and individual potentialities of people. This is the crux of the DNA model of TM. However, DNA model of TM has been explained by different

Figure 5.2
Talent on Demand Model

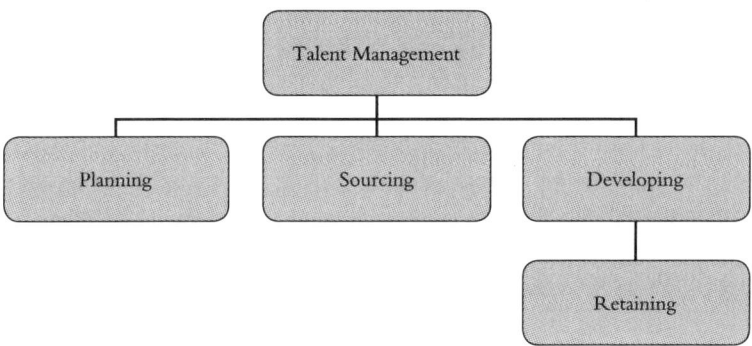

scholars differently. The generic DNA model rests on following three premises:

- Generic skills and capabilities required throughout the organization.
- Specific skills and capabilities related to various job positions.
- Ability of the organizations to meet both the requirements hiring right people.

With the above three generic focus, effective TM is possible as organization can successfully balance the demand and supply of talent through recruitment, onboarding, and employee development.

Models on TM widely vary across the organizations, for lack of universality in TM concepts. Browsing literatures on TM, we find following definitions are better accepted in terms of organizational practices. For example, Cappelli (2008a) defined TM as the process of anticipating and meeting the needs of human capital. Davies and Davies (2010) viewed TM as a systematic process of attracting, identifying, developing, engaging/retaining, and deploying high potential people who can add value to the organization. Lewis and Heckman (2006), realizing the problem in defining TM in unambiguous way, recommended three streams of thoughts to understand TM processes in organizations. First, TM is human capital management. Second, TM is a process to ensure adequate flow of quality manpower throughout the organization. And finally, TM focuses on generic talent, rather than talent within the organization per se.

Final Take

TM models are specific to organizational requirements. As organizations prefer in their business focus, strategies, and business priorities, develop their own TM model.

Managing talent: Lessons from McDonalds

In recent years McDonalds lost four CEOs, primarily for illness and premature death. The effect was evident from poor performance of the company. To overcome such problems in future, the company today operates with a robust TM team with specific mandates on enhancement of performance, improvement of succession planning and in-house talent development and Leadership at McDonalds program (LAMP). TM systems have now become more inclusive, as its scope now even extended to non-executive job positions, so as to develop in-house talent pipeline, to meet any eventualities in future.

With a mission to be a customers' favorite place to eat and drink, the company focus on building a great place to work with positive culture of quality, service, cleanliness, customers' value. McDonald's talent management practices are embedded in their commitment to lifelong learning for all cross-sections of employees, so that either they can grow in present job or can equip them for a future role in the company. The company's TM program therefore is grounded on the career development of all employees. Career development at McDonalds is more encompassing, as it covers career planning, individual development plans, career maps, succession planning, and learning activities. Aligned with organizational TM objectives, career development program of McDonalds helps in talent retention also. With diversity and inclusion as part of their culture, the company now makes their TM process more robust with a talent pipeline, built on their in-house capabilities.

Return on Investment from TM

In a competitive market for talent, organizations invest in talent with a futuristic outlook. With an effective talent pipeline, organizations can meet their future talent requirements also to sustain and grow. But it is also important to assess the ROI from such TM pursuits of the organizations. Approaches to measurement of ROI from talent widely vary across the organizations. For example, to measure ROI, most of the organizations focus on measuring their investment on all talent development activities, like succession, retention, engagement, internal promotions, and diversity. Only some organizations extend such ROI calculation to performance measures, revenue, profit margin, and productivity. Some of the empirical studies on the process of ROI calculation for TM (Parry & Tyson, 2007) identified following common measures:

- total cost of TM programs;
- average cost of TM programs;
- cost of TM against retention of talent;
- cost of talent against alternative approaches to career progression;
- cost of talent against productivity; and
- relative cost of various TM techniques.

These measures hardly emphasize on other important HR ratios or metrics, rather more specific to assess the top line (revenue) and bottom line (margin) effect of investment on TM.

Organizations' desire to invest in talent is primarily driven by reasons, like shortage of talent, responding to competition for talent, developing talent pipeline, and transforming organization to a talent driven one. On the other hand, when organizations choose not to invest in talent, suffer in achieving the business goals. Thus, investing in TM enhances the organization's brand value, and with such enhanced brand value, organizations can attract and retain talent.

In calculating ROI from talent or TM, it is always advisable not to strictly measure in terms of cost-benefit analysis, rather consider whether such investment delivering value to the business of the organization. For example, customer retention is possible, when employee retention is high. Customers feel more comfortable in dealing with same employee of the organization, because of the relationship effect. Now this cannot be explained in cost-benefit terms, but certainly it is an important effect or outcome of investment in talent. Many scholars and professionals argue that as long as investment in talent bring positive changes in employees' performance, and enable the organization to stay with the strategy, the long-term effect being meaningful, we consider it meaningful.

In designing a TM framework for an organization, we emphasize on people alignment with the job roles. Such alignment is ensured by the organizations from two different perspectives. Hence, both the perspectives deserve careful considerations in managing talent for the organization. For example, HR functions, like recruitment, onboarding, promotion, career planning and development, succession planning, and learning and development help in aligning people with their job roles. Similarly, organizations also strive to align job roles to people, focusing on organizational design, job description, compensation and rewards, work process, and work environment. Such alignment for its integrative effect can help in realizing the benefits of TM programs and justify the ROI from TM.

For C-suite

Learning TM from Google

Google is one of those organizations, which could realize the importance of TM to sustain and grow in a competitive work environment. For sourcing new talents, and even for incubating talent from within, the company excelled in their TM practices. In fact the company even goes for acquisition spree like Apple and Yahoo to acquire talent, not just for extending the business value chain. Globally number of studies authenticated the

(Box continued)

(Box continued)

difference between good and bad performances, mediated by talent is 100 to 1. This syndrome is more evident in critical jobs. And Google as a company is engaged more in innovative and critical jobs. Google recruits people who have critical knowledge base and skills, and then assign them to critical job roles, facilitate their development with free time to pursue their pet projects, reinforce their knowledge and skill through continuous learning and development, and transform them to top talent. Such a talent-driven culture could make it possible for the company to sustain and grow in highly competitive market.

How Do We Identify People Are Talented

ROI from TM is not the only possible way for assessing the success of organizational effort for TM. All organizations cannot emulate the practices of Google, that is, recruiting the people with existing talent, and then developing them further through in-house reinforcements. Again, process of in-house incubation of talent also varies across the organizations. Keeping in mind all these variations, a quantitative index to measure the efficacy of TM programs of the organizations can be developed as under:

- positive change in performance index;
- positive change in total factor productivity index;
- positive change in business results in terms of top line (revenue);
- positive change in business results in terms of bottom line (profit);
- increase in employee retention rate;
- increase in employees' capability in undertaking critical projects;
- increase in employees' capacity to relate;
- increase in employees' capacity to work;
- increase in employees' identity with the organization; and
- increase in employees' innovation.

Hence, using this quantitative index, organizations can measure efficacy of their TM programs.

Final Take

In a competitive market for talent, organizations invest in talent with a futuristic outlook.

Approaches to measurement of ROI from talent widely vary across the organizations.

Investment in TM enhances the organization's brand value, and with such enhanced brand value, organizations can attract and retain talent.

In designing a TM framework for an organization, we emphasize on people alignment with the job roles. Such alignment can help in realizing the benefits of TM programs, and justify the ROI from TM.

ROI from TM is not the only possible way for assessing the success of organizational effort for TM.

Strategic TM

Managing talent strategically at the outset requires organization to recognize that talent is the most important strategic force for organizational success. A recent CIPD (2014) study even states that only 17 percent of the organizations have integrated TM process, and they believe talent is strategically important for organizations. The survey was conducted in UK covering more than 40 large organizations, with 2.5 million people in their payroll. This itself speaks organizations are yet to attach any importance to TM, and continue with their age-old activity-based HRM functions. We have already discussed at length the concepts of TM. When we talk about strategic TM, we mean all activities spanning the life cycle of employees, which help us to develop them, make them capable, encourage them to innovate, take risk, and perform at exceed expectation level. Like the perceptions on talent and TM, organizations also differ in their approaches to strategic TM. For example, Cappelli (2008b) suggested to identify of critical talent in organizations and then invest for creating new opportunities for the organizations to grow. Contrarily, Taleo observed TM in general is a strategy. Taleo Corporation primarily offers talent acquisition software, known as "Talent Intelligence." This software can also be used in performance management, learning, and development, and compensation management. With effect from February 9, 2012, the company has been acquired by Oracle Corporation. The talent management software of Taleo is most extensively used across the world. Difference in these two approaches clarify that whether organizations consider their TM function strategic or not is more left to their choice and HRM practices. However, organizations with a long-term business focus must consider TM strategically.

Organizations which have embraced the idea of managing talent strategically evidently streamline their TM processes, with focus on following aspects:

- identification and assessment of new and existing talent;
- grooming the talent pool;
- maintaining a high level of engagement throughout an employee's tenure;
- retention of the talent pool; and
- maintaining adequate bench strength.

Such focus, however, simultaneously requires alignment with the core objectives of the organization on TM. Again core objectives of the organizations on TM may vary. Some generic core objectives of TM, which need to be aligned with the strategic focus of TM in the organization, are listed below:

- Strategic retention and development of talent.
- Building a sustainable talent pipeline for maintaining flow of talent in the organization.
- Designing competitive compensation and rewards program.
- Promoting employee engagement.

When companies subscribe to such TM objectives, it is possible to manage TM strategically, and derive benefits from the TM program. However, time and resource constraints often dissuade organization to adopt ad hoc approach in managing talent. Hence, CIPD survey is an eye opener for us.

Two Indian companies which are internationally acclaimed for strategic TM programs are ICICI Bank and HUL. The survey was jointly conducted by the RBL Group and Hewitt Associates (2009). In fact ICICI Bank is ranked 5th and Hindustan Unilever is ranked 10th in strategic TM practices, out of top 25 companies of the world "for Leaders." IBM, Procter & Gamble, and General Mills are ranked respectively as 1st, 2nd, and 3rd. Another Indian company, ranked as 24th out of 25 companies of the world is Infosys. Such encouraging scenario of TM practices among Indian companies and figuring in global map, however, does not speak about our general consensus on the need for embracing strategic TM. Series of studies conducted by many globally known consulting organizations indicate poor state of TM practices in Indian organizations.

Some of the practicing evidences on strategic TM of these top ranking companies are listed below:

- alignment with strategy;
- involvement of the top;
- creation of talent pipeline;
- ongoing leadership/talent development programs;
- ongoing TM;
- structured behavioral pattern and HR practices;
- putting talent in the list of critical objective of the organization;
- integrative approach to TM; and
- institutionalization of TM practices in organizations.

For HR managers

How do you align people with TM strategy?

Aligning people with the TM strategy is the most important part of TM function. With inputs from different verticals of the

(Box continued)

(Box continued)

organization, at the outset identify capability/competency gaps of the people. For better decisional accuracy, if required interpret the performance records. Assess your present and future talent (capability/competency) needs, and then identify talent gaps. Categorize talent job wise and draw plans for learning and development programs to meet present talent gap. Reinforce it with mentoring and coaching programs. Draw development plans for meeting the future talent gap. Based on your organizational strategy, make it either exclusive or inclusive. Simultaneously reinforce your TM programs with succession plans, career plans, and retention plans. Develop competitive compensation and reward plans, and employee engagement plans.

Final Take

Managing talent strategically at the outset requires organization to recognize that talent is the most important strategic force for organizational success.

Like the perceptions on talent and TM, organizations also differ in their approaches to strategic TM.

Organizations which have embraced the idea of managing talent strategically are evidently able to streamline their TM processes.

TM Practices

TM practices vary across the organizations due to difference in strategic perspectives. This has already been discussed. Even then we must have some ground rule for TM practices to achieve operational objectives with an organization. Practices being the expected way of doing something, TM practices help in understanding the activities to be performed so that it can lead to desired results. As per Morton, Ashton, and Bellis (2005), TM practices encompass following areas in an organization.

- recruitment;
- retention;

- professional development;
- leadership/high potential development;
- performance management;
- feedback/measurement;
- workforce planning; and
- culture.

Out of these, recruitment, development, and retention are considered as the key TM practices, which are universal in nature. Using the talent life cycle, we can explain the universal TM practices as under:

- plan;
- acquire;
- develop;
- deploy;
- retain; and
- evaluate.

Thus, TM practices need to be aligned with the strategic plan of the organizations, so that it can successfully address the business needs, and facilitate in transforming the organization to a talent driven one. This means TM practices need to be more proactive, well-orchestrated, and business driven.

Strategic Global Talent Management

Organizations that have global operations need to adopt a global approach to TM. Globalization has increased the agility of people and talent is increasingly becoming borderless. Talented people can move to any country located anywhere for their rewarding careers. Organizations in cross-border mergers are particularly facing the challenge of global TM. The Belgian chemical major Solvay after acquiring Rhodia of France substantially reshaped their business portfolio, changing the market spread to countries like China and others in Southeast Asia. The company could meet their talent constraint in such markets, first setting up global business units (GBUs), and then developing local managers/talents to run the business. Even sourcing local talents and developing them to work for the organization is a challenging task in China. The company achieves this by offering to local talents rewarding and exciting career and with opportunities to acquire new skills and knowledge. Such practice in global TM is totally a different phenomenon, as even in recent past, companies used to meet their talent requirements in countries, other than their own origin, deputing managers from head quarters. Even today we find Japanese organizations follow this.

Relocating talents to international locations is one possible age-old practice of global TM. But various cross-cultural issues often defeat such purpose, leading to organizational failure to sustain in global market. Obviously for such reason, developing local talents, for international operations, is considered as the best TM strategy.

Another important issue in global TM strategy is organization's sourcing of talents from international market for the critical skill sets. This is particularly important in cases of knowledge intensive organizations, and IT enabled services. HR managers along with their HR operations additionally need to manage such expatriate talents, addressing various cross-cultural issues. Depending on the expatriate's tenure of employment, strategically organizations decide the nature and extent of TM activities. The process of alignment of expatriate talents with the organizations business goals and strategies hinders when such assignees come for a shorter duration to undertake specific critical tasks.

Global talent mobility has also increased the competition for talent in the local market. For example, Towers Watson Study (2013) indicate Indian organizations, realizing the strategic importance of talent, now benchmark their TM practices, including rewards and compensation with global organizations. With globally competitive rewards and compensation, and proactive TM practices, Indian organizations are able to reduce global mobility of talents from their organizations.

Your Take—For C-suite

Make your global talent more culture sensitive

Professor Andy Molinsky (2013) in his world famous book on Global Dexterity has documented six important cultural variables. These variables we can also consider for global talents. Your organizations must sensitize your global talents on these aspects, so that they are effective in their communication while executing their cross-cultural role.

- Directness—straightforwardness in communication
- Enthusiasm—demonstration of emotion and energy while communicating
- Formality—exposition of deference and respect while communicating
- Assertiveness—degree of forthrightness in communication
- Self-promotion—positively communicating about oneself
- Personal disclosure—degree of openness in sharing personal details while communicating

All the above variables can be studied in high–low continuum. A US manager on deputation to India will find it seemingly difficult to communicate as in all the above constructs they are in high continuum against India, except in "formality" constructs, where India is ahead of the United States.

Final Take

TM practices vary across the organizations due to differences in strategic perspectives.

Practices being the expected way of doing something, TM practices help in understanding the activities to be performed so that it can lead to desired results.

TM practices need to be aligned with the strategic plan of the organizations, so that it can successfully address the business needs, and facilitate in transforming the organization to a talent driven one.

(Box continued)

(Box continued)

> Organizations that have global operations need to adopt a global approach to TM.
> In cross-border mergers organizations particularly face the challenge of global TM.
> Relocating talents to international locations is one possible age-old practice of global TM. But various cross-cultural issues often defeat such purpose, leading to organizational failure to sustain in global market. Obviously for such reason, developing local talents, for international operations, is considered as the best TM strategy.

TM Scenario in Indian Organizations

Making the right pitch for the right people is the mantra of Indian organizations in TM. However, such organizations are few in numbers. Companies like Lenovo India, Fortis Global Healthcare Holdings, Columbia Asia Hospitals, Real Estate Company Puravankara, Aditya Birla Group, all have pledged for TM practices, and the top management of these companies directly involves them in TM. Earlier we have described the case of three Indian companies, that is, ICICI Bank, HUL, and Infosys, who had topped in their TM initiatives globally. Aidan Brennan, the global head of management consulting practice of KPMG in a recent interview with the *Economic Times* (Shelley Singh, ET Bureau. There's a talent crisis globally but not in India, says Aidan Brennan of KPMG, http://articles.economictimes.indiatimes.com/2014-05-10/news/49757846_1_supply-chain-data-analytics-kpmg [accessed on April 11, 2015], May 10, 2014), expressed that in India does not have talent shortage. In one way we may feel complacent, as we do not require investing in TM programs, but reality is far from truth. Many Indian companies are talent starved and for the critical jobs they depend on migrants. Therefore, systematic TM approach is recommended for all organizations, irrespective of the fact whether they have business presence globally or not.

Some of the important drivers that influenced TM functions in India are:

- Rapid technological changes throughout the world, among others changed the fundamental relationship between people and work.
- Increased spate of competition in domestic and international market.
- Increase in quality and price competition due to consumerism, government regulation, and international competition.
- Increase in social interface of the organizations, enhancing society's stake with the organization.
- Responsible trade unionism.
- Change in knowledge and skill profile of the jobs.

Indian organizations which have been successful in understanding such TM triggers could introduce TM practices to ensure their sustainability and growth.

Final Take

Many Indian companies are talent starved and for the critical jobs they depend on the migrants.

Rapid technological changes throughout the world, among others changed the fundamental relationship between people and work in Indian organizations also.

Indian organizations which have been successful in understanding TM triggers could introduce TM practices to ensure their sustainability and growth.

Talent management: Story of NTPC India

"People before PLF (Plant Load Factor)" is NTPC's declared HR philosophy, which is evident from their commitment to development of employees. With 26,000 headcounts, NTPC is now

(Box continued)

(Box continued)

the largest power and energy company in India with best focus on TM and talent-driven work culture. NTPC's HR systems are built around four building blocks—competence, commitment, culture, and systems. With HR vision of transforming people to world class professionals, the company believes in the philosophy of "Grow your own timber." With the objective of developing home grown talents, the company introduced 52 weeks' induction training for all new recruits. NTPC's TM systems rest on performance management, career paths and leadership development. TM systems of the company further get reinforced with the culture of rewards and recognitions, culture of "innovate, create, compete," and quality of work life. Strong knowledge management, training and development support, education upgradation schemes, seeking feedback, and awards, further strengthened the TM systems of NTPC, transforming it truly to a talent-driven organization.

Managing Talent with Big Data

Big data, which so far was used for strategic and marketing decisions in organizations, is now becoming popular for use in TM. This is what we call talent analytics. Using talent analytics, organizations can effectively manage TM function, particularly in predicting the potential talents, their performance, etc. Simultaneously TM functions can become more scientific and data driven, resulting objective decisions in hiring or recruiting new talents, in identifying potential talents within the organization and design their succession plans. Also, this helps in designing suitable rewards and compensation for talented employees for their retention, in drawing career progression path for the identified talents, and finally also in designing talent development programs for building the talent pipeline.

Let us understand talent analytics with an example from the corporate world. A company while hiring new talents makes assumptions that those who are from top B-schools are expected to be good performers and can groom themselves for future leadership role in the organizations. Such assumption makes the company prepare a list of handful of B-schools where they might visit to recruit. The company has made this assumption based on their past performance data of recruitees from top B-schools. Some companies may also have differential rewards and compensation packages for newly hired talents from different B-schools. Such assumptions again based on their past performance assessment of B-schools graduates. Opposed to this some companies may only account for the experience of B-schools graduates. Most of the top B-schools only admit experienced undergraduates in their MBA programs. Based on the previous performance track record, they try to assess, using predictive analytics, to what extent such new recruits would be able to achieve success in achieving the performance results. With the type of experience they are already exposed to, would they be able to add value to their new place of employment.

However, we have many critics who dissuade us from the use of talent analytics. It cannot replace the managerial thought process and belief systems with which the organizations are working for ages together. Some scholars, however, contradict this, as companies truly dissuade them from data based HRM decisions, which also encompass TM. They consider big data or talent analytics is an opportunity, and organizations must explore the same.

Talent analytics can help organizations to predict performance of the new hires, reduce the employee attrition, align TM with business and strategies of the organization, make organization a talent-driven one, and transform organization for long-term sustainability and growth. However, having talent analytics, without changing the mindset to data-based decision making, may defeat the purpose of such predictive tool of decision making. This has also been admitted by many major Talent Analytics vendors. This is why some scholars also recommend with big data, we must use our big insights for effective TM.

Organizations while choosing the talent analytics suite from software vendors first consider the degree of its relevance to specific business situations. What would be its impact in terms of its returns from investment? Can the analytics also suggest action? Finally, for achieving degree of fit in terms of relevance, optimize ROI for better impact, and ability to recommend courses of action, we also need to streamline the right perspectives of the anchors of TM functions of the organizations. Without the right perspectives, talent leaders will fail to raise the right questions and assess what data are necessary to answer such questions (which may often be irrelevant).

To ensure effective utilization of talent analytics, it is recommended that analytics should also factor business data, in addition to the HR data. It also must consider performance outcomes, that is, the effect. Some measurable results in terms of enhanced performance, reduced attrition, etc., should be there to legitimize its use.

Final Take

Big data, which so far was used for strategic and marketing decisions in organizations, is now becoming popular for use in TM. This is what we call talent analytics.

Using talent analytics, organizations can effectively manage TM function, particularly in predicting the potential talents, their performance, etc.

Also talent analytics help in designing suitable rewards and compensation for talented employees for their retention, in drawing career progression path for the identified talents, and finally also in designing talent development programs for building the talent pipeline.

However, talent analytics cannot replace the managerial thought process and belief systems with which the organizations are working for ages together.

Organizations while choosing the talent analytics suite from software vendors first consider the degree of its relevance to specific business situations.

To ensure effective utilization of talent analytics, it is recommended that analytics should also factor business data, in addition to the HR data.

Operational Issues in TM and Performance Management Systems (PMS)

Most important operational issue is integrating PMS of the organization with the TM. Hence, while managing talent, we need to carefully study each aspect of PMS to understand the talent availability and gap, and to design suitable talent development programs. Also effective PMS help in identifying the potential talents, and in this process facilitate the succession plans for developing the robust talent pipeline. But first we need to understand why PMS is important for TM?

PMS is now acknowledged as the strategic HRM function, as apart from its use as the basis of important HR decisions, like compensation and rewards, promotion, demotion, transfer, and identification of training needs, it also helps in identifying the potential talents in the organizations. Well-designed PMS can further help in TM functions, identifying talent gap, and then deciding on the talent development programs for the organization. It is therefore the responsibility of talent managers to integrate PMS with the TM functions.

PMS as a catalyst to TM starts from core job descriptions reinforced with strategic plans and goals, which translates to performance development, performance appraisal, observations and feedback, and reformulating the performance standards. This cycle continues, as performance management is an ongoing employee development function.

For integrating PMS with the TM systems of the organizations, at the outset we must believe in strategic dimensions of HRM functions. This autonomously makes HRM functions business aligned, of which TM is an important part. This also helps in adopting an integrated approach to develop the competencies of employees, identification of talents in terms of performance results, assessment of training and development needs, designing development plans, designing rewards and compensation packages, and finally designing future career developing plans. All these are important part of TM functions.

Further integration of TM with PMS would be possible when both the employees and the managers mutually feel responsible to communicate performance, develop performance targets, and design the PMS. The organization must also feel responsible to design and develop a transparent PMS. This can motivate employees to deliver their best, helping the organization to identify the potential talents, and can also provide desired inputs for effective TM functions.

Thus, the espoused values and beliefs of effective PMS when positive, can motivate the employees to deliver their best. It helps in manifesting potential talents in the organization, and provides inputs for effective TM functions.

TM Compensation and Rewards

Compensation and rewards programs of organization play the most crucial role in attracting and retaining talent in the organization. For many organizations, compensation and rewards programs are the major differentiator for effective TM functions. Over the years mobility of talented people, across organizations, has increased manifold. Cross-border hiring, cross-industry hiring, and even talent poaching have now almost become a regular pursuits of organizations. Global companies like CISCO, Apple, Microsoft, Yahoo, Google often acquire companies just to get talented people in their payroll, rather than focusing on increasing their value chain of product portfolio through acquisition. For talent, organizations focus on strategic HRM practices. First among such strategies is employer branding. Successful employer branding, radiates the image of the employer in the minds of the people, and as a natural process attracts the potential talent for the organization. Employer branding is the result of proactive HRM practices, which include compensating employees based on talent.

Talent is the people value which contributes to the success of any organization. A talented person through innovation enhances the competitive strength of organization. Competency-based HRM practices, have lately institutionalized TM in organizations.

Talent is now the key driver of organizational success and suste-nance. A talent-driven organization focuses on building the future leadership pipeline through various human resource develop-ment (HRD) and organizational development (OD) initiatives. However, institutionalized TM practices, among others, require organizations to align their compensation policies and plans. Hence, in crafting TM strategy, organizations now also emphasize on integration of their compensation policies and strategies. This ensures attraction and retention of talent, incubating talent, and ultimately making the organization talent driven. It is for this we need to understand compensation management issues that encom-pass effective TM in organization. Importance of compensation for integrated TM encompasses job evaluation, market surveys for external benchmarking data, competencies, work measurement, identification of organizational key performance indicators (KPI), corresponding key performance areas (KRA) of employees, and internal benchmarking to assess internal equity, etc. All these when considered can ensure compensation design to attract and retain talent, and cascade to effective TM.

Merit-based pay, performance-related pay, innovative stock options, broad-based rewards and incentive plan, and provisions for deferred benefits, and perquisites are all monetary compensa-tion components used especially for effective TM in organizations. Apart from these, organizations also emphasize on suitable non-monetary compensation components, like investing on learning and development opportunities, vacation plan, etc.

Some of the recommended practices for compensation inte-grated TM practices are listed below.

- *Incentivize and motivate high performing workers:* This can ensure attraction, development, and retention of talent in organi-zation. Some of the innovative incentivization policies are performance-based incentive plans, incentivization based on merit, decision on incentive-mix both monetary and non-monetary, etc. Incentivization must be tuned with the expectations of employees. For this many organizations adopt flexible incentivization policies, responding to the inputs received from the talented employees. However, it requires organization to ensure overall spread of compensation is well within the strategies of the organizations.

- *Designing compensation to drive business results:* Compensation for effective TM may often create inequity in the organizations. As long as such inequitable compensation outweigh revenue and profit growth for the organization, it can be sustained for talented employees. However, organizations may be required to consider the possible deteriorating effect on motivation and performance levels of other employees. It is for this reason more emphasis on variables, contingent upon performance is given, keeping the door open for all cross-section of employees. This will not impair the overall compensation plan for the companies. While companies decide on standard compensation based on their strategies and business goals, considering the job roles, market data and internal pay ranges, for talented employees, focus is more on performance-based pay with KPIs, such as achievement of goal, performance ratings, and non-quantitative measures. Non-quantitative measures assess outcome of employees' performance, that is, the effect that the employees leave behind in achieving their performance results.

Strategic Compensation and Talent Issues in Global Hiring

With the increased shortage of talent, organizations today compete for global talent. Talent is increasingly becoming the major differentiator for organizational success and sustenance, organizations with long-term perspective also navigate world for hiring the talented people. For global hiring of talent, organizations try to understand the implication of their strategic compensation decisions. For example, the US-based multinational companies, which emphasize on more and more variables, aligning with the performance of their employees, may not apparently find any difficulty in attracting and retaining talent. But for Indian talents, their strategic compensation design may not work. This is because of cultural incongruence. Indian employees, and also the talents still value the fixed compensation component. They make those organizations as their second choice, which focus on performance-related pay or variables. This problem is particularly faced by the multinationals that have their business presence across the globe. For instance, Solvay and Pentair, two European multinationals have gone for change in their business focus. Such change through acquisitions has not only changed their business portfolio but also their market reach. Biggest challenge that these two organizations faced recently is to transfer talented managerial manpower to their international operations for a longer duration, more for the issues related to culture and compensation cost-effectiveness. Both the companies then started incubating local managerial talents in their GBUs.

Employers around the world are focused on attracting, retaining, and motivating key talent, but according to experts, the complexities of varied cultures and global economies means many employers are struggling with the details. Apart from the cultural issues that influence the strategic compensation design for global talent hiring, organizations also face the challenge to invest in training and career planning. The challenge is optimizing the cost of compensation, yet achieve success in hiring global talent, strategic compensation management focuses on following important points:

- Reinforce PRP with logical distribution of weights, balancing between individual and collective achievement of goals.
- Engage people in deciding on the elements of compensation, as there may be every possibility that some compensation elements may not be the right fit in a particular country or culture. For example, Cisco's employee benefits program consists of multiple options. But some of the benefits of Cisco are not globally offered, it is restricted to some specific place or location.
- Communicate the compensation plan to people, else people will smell something fishy. Communication can ensure transparency, and at the same time, employees can also get their clarifications, if at all required.

In designing compensation strategy, wherever required we may follow the segmented reward strategy, but at the same time we need to be careful about too much inequity, which may frustrate the dormant talent to continue with the organization.

International Compensation Strategies for Talent engagement

With McKinsey's study on "War for Talent" (Chambers et al., 1998), organizations globally started renewing their focus on talent engagement and retention through effective compensation strategies. To manage talent, in practice, organizations follow two approaches—differentiating and inclusive. Differentiating approach means organizations focus only on those employees who are indentified talent, that is, who are having high value and potentiality over others. Such identified talent gets more attention in terms of resource support, training, increased compensation, etc. However, globally we also find organizations, who adopt inclusive approach, that is, focusing on all cross-sections of employees. In the first case, organizations try to achieve excellence through top performers, while in the second case, organizations try to institutionalize the culture of performance, making every one competent through effective TM activities. Differentiated approach to TM has been initially practiced by GE, and today we find many organizations across the globe practice this. Companies like Shell, and in India Murugappa Group follow inclusive approach.

Whatever may be the approach to talent engagement, international compensation strategies, adopted by the organizations, focus on the following principles:

- alignment of the compensation plan with business strategy of the organization;
- valuing internal equity;
- valuing culture;
- top-down approach;

- balancing between global and local needs; and
- focus on organizational branding for talent attraction.

These are generic principles for talent engagement at international level, through compensation strategies. However, firms may individually follow their own tools and techniques to engage talent, using other HRM practices.

Final Take

Effective PMS help in identifying the potential talents and in this process facilitate the succession plans for developing the robust talent pipeline.

PMS as a catalyst to TM starts from core job descriptions reinforced with strategic plans and goals, which translates to performance development, performance appraisal, observations and feedback, and reformulating the performance standards.

Integration of TM with PMS would be possible when both the employees and the managers mutually feel responsible to communicate performance, develop performance targets, and design the PMS.

Like PMS compensation and rewards programs of organization play the most crucial role in attracting and retaining talent in the organization.

Employer branding is the result of proactive HRM practices, which include compensating employees based on talent.

For global hiring of talents, organizations try to understand the implication of their strategic compensation decisions, in terms of cultural constructs.

Summing up

This final chapter of the book wrapped up with elaborate discussions on TM issues, referring to TM practices. All the preceding chapters discussed on specific TM areas, like acquisition, retention, and development.

As an integrated HRM function, primary activities of TM are attracting, acquiring, developing, and retaining right people for the right job at the right time. Effective TM needs to be business aligned and strategy focused, and effective TM can enhance competitive advantage of the organization. Change in business processes and change in technology together culminate change in the TM process of the organization. In designing a TM framework for an organization, we emphasize on people alignment with the job roles. Such alignment can help in realizing the benefits of TM programs, and justify the ROI from TM.

TM practices need to be aligned with the strategic plan of the organizations, so that it can successfully address the business needs, and facilitate in transforming the organization to a talent driven one. Organizations having global operations need to adopt a global approach to TM. In cross-border mergers organizations are particularly facing the challenge of global TM.

Many Indian companies are talent starved and for the critical jobs they depend on the migrants. Big data, which so far was used for strategic and marketing decisions in organizations, are now becoming popular for use in TM. This is what we call talent analytics. Using talent analytics, organizations can effectively manage TM function, particularly in predicting the potential talents, their performance, etc.

Also talent analytics help in designing suitable rewards and compensation for talented employees for their retention, in drawing career progression path for the identified talents, and finally also in designing talent development programs for building the talent pipeline.

Effective PMS help in identifying the potential talents and in this process facilitate the succession plans for developing the robust talent pipeline. For global hiring of talents, organizations try to understand the implication of their strategic compensation decisions, in terms of cultural constructs.

Duality in Compensation Management Practices for Talent Retention: Case of CISCO

Cisco Systems, a global networking company, for successive years has been reducing its manpower. In July 24, 2012, Cisco announced its plan to prune manpower reducing 1,300 jobs. Cisco estimated this would enable them to save around US$1 billion, that is, the cost of compensation and benefits for these 1,300 jobs. The year before, that is, in July 2011, Cisco phased out 10,000 jobs. The company attributes it to their ongoing austerity program. This job cut will help Cisco to save around US$1 billion in a year, and adjust its position to changing economic conditions. Cisco is able to sustain such job-cuts, as in every move they simplify their operations. From a figure of 75,000 strong workforces, Cisco had to optimize their workforce to 65,000, that is, almost reducing their manpower to 14 percent.

Cisco's example is a unique lesson for manpower analysts across the globe. With such successive cut in manpower, Cisco sustained with a marginal drop in their profitability. Many analysts feel Cisco always tried to retain their profit margin, adjusting it against the market volatility, making their workers as the first casualty. Along with this job cut, Cisco also had an early retirement package.

Frequent manpower curtailment helped Cisco to save on their compensation cost, although Cisco's Chief Executive Officer John Chambers attributed frequent job slashing to exit less profitable businesses due to increase in number of competitors, who are able to offer price efficient products.

Although manpower curtailment for cost-cutting, saving the cost of compensation had become almost a regular feature for Cisco, the company is also known for compensation design for their executives, even above the market average. The 1984 company with current headcount of 65,223 is now operating from 420 locations of 93 countries. Their employees are broadly categorized in Engineering, Sales, and other business functions. Engineering represents

(Case Study continued)

(Case Study continued)

33.8 percent of Cisco's workforce, followed by Sales (25.5 percent), and other business functions (40.7 percent). The benefits package for employees of Cisco is quite elaborate, and most of these benefits are also offered for Indian employees. The company even goes for acquisition, not for adding to their value stream, but to acquire talent.

Thus, Cisco is a perfect company to practice duality in compensation management, for its best strategic use for the growth and sustainability.

Bibliography

Barney, J. B., & Wright, P. M. (1998). On becoming a strategic partner: The role of human resources in gaining competitive advantage. *Human Resource Management, 37*, 31–46.

Baruch, Y. (2004). *Managing careers: Theory and practice.* Harlow: FT Prentice Hall.

———. (2010). *Cross-cultural management: Text and cases.* New Delhi: PHI Learning.

———. (2011). *Performance management systems and strategies.* New Delhi: Pearson.

———. (2014). *Compensation management* (2nd ed.). New Delhi: Oxford University Press.

Cappelli, P. (2008a). *Talent on demand.* Boston, MA: Harvard Business Press.

———. (2008b). Talent management for the twenty-first century. *Harvard Business Review, 86*, 74–81.

Chambers, E. G., Foulon, M., Handfield-Jones, H., Hankin, S. M., & Michaels, E. G. (1998). The war for talent. *McKinsey Quarterly, 3*, 44–57.

Chartered Institute of Personnel and Development (CIPD). (2014). *Talent management: An overview.* London: CIPD.

Davies, B., & Davies, B. J. (2010). Talent management in academies. *International Journal of Educational Management, 24*, 418–426.

Freeman, R. B., & Katz, L. F. (1994). Rising wage inequality: The United States vs. other advanced countries. In R. Freeman (Ed.), *Working under different rules.* New York: Russell Sage Foundation and NBER, pp. 29–62.

Hofstede, G. (1983). The cultural relativity of organizational practices and theories. *Journal of International Business Studies, 14*, 75–89.

Lewis, R. E., & Heckman, R. J. (2006). Talent management: A critical review. *Human Resource Management Review, 16*, 139–154.

Molinsky, A. (2013). *Global dexterity.* Harvard: Harvard Business Review Press.

Morton, L., Ashton, C., & Bellis, R. (2005). *Differentiating talent management: Integrating talent management to drive business performance*. London: CRF Publishing.

Parry, E., & Tyson, S. (2007). *UK talent report*. Cranfield: Cranfield School of Management, Human Resources Research Centre.

RBL Group and Hewitt Associates. (2009). Study http://internationalhrforum. com/2010/04/08/how-top-companies-manage-talent-development/#sthash.0Y9Q049V.dpuf

Towers Watson Study. (2013). Talent management & rewards India report. www.towerswatson.com/en-IN/Insights/IC-Types/Survey-Research-Results/2013/06/Talent-Management-and-Rewards-Study-India-Report (accessed on April 16, 2015).

About the Author

Dipak Kumar Bhattacharyya is a Professor of Organizational Behavior at Xavier Institute of Management, Bhubaneswar, India. He is Ph.D. in Management from University of Calcutta, West Bengal, India. For about 15 years, he has served the corporate world in training and organizational development function. In the last two decades, he has worked with several management institutes in India. He has also served as the Director, Centre for Management Education, All India Management Association, New Delhi; the Director (Academic), Institute of Engineering and Management, Kolkata; and a Dean, Indian Institute of Social Welfare and Business Management, Kolkata. He is a visiting faculty at XLRI—Xavier School of Management, Jamshedpur. Professor Bhattacharyya has an extensive consultancy experience in human resources (HR), quality management, and organizational development and restructuring areas. He has published 25 books on HR management, and has contributed more than 100 papers in various journals of national and international repute.